LNER WAGONS

Peter Tatlow

PENDRAGON

LNER WAGONS

AN ILLUSTRATED OVERVIEW

Peter Tatlow

PENDRAGON

To fellow members of the LNER Study Group

ISBN 1 899816 05 4

Printed by the Amadeus Press Ltd., Huddersfield, West Yorkshire

Published by the Pendragon Partnership,
PO Box No.3, Easingwold, York YO6 3YS

Front top left
A 12 ton 17ft 6in long 10 foot wheelbase covered goods
van No 175829 fitted with automatic vacuum brake, as
well as lever operated hand brake. This vehicle has an
early version of the pressed steel corrugated ends
without the ventilating bonnet more usual on later and
slightly narrower bodied vans, see page 35 and 36. This
van appears to be new construction in July 1934,
probably at Shildon Works. (BR)

Front top right
A plywood bodied 4 ton Type B covered container
No BC620 on a container flat No 175953 in July 1935.
The development in covered and open containers of
various types and sizes, together with the vehicles upon
which they were loaded, to convey the considerable
increase in such traffic is discussed on pages 69 to 75. (BR)

Front bottom
The LNER had only two styles of standard goods brake
van, both of 20 tons. The more readily identified with
company was the 24 foot long 16 foot wheelbase vans,
but with only 16ft 3in long bodies built for the increasing
number of full brake fitted express goods trains being
introduced by the LNER. This is exemplified here by
No 235109 built in August 1939. Further examples will
be found on pages 167 to 169. (BR)

Rear
During the early years of its existence, before
conveyance by road made large inroads into the traffic,
the LNER built substantial numbers of 19 foot long fitted
and unfitted large category cattle trucks on timber
underframes with a 9 foot wheelbase. No 153516 was
built at Doncaster in October 1928. As well as the screw
couplings and vacuum brake hoses, note the steam pipe
to enable the van to be worked by passenger train
during the colder months of the year. (NRM)

CONTENTS

A shortage of suitable timber leading up to the war led to the adoption of eight, instead of the more usual seven planks to the side of this 12 ton end door mineral wagon No 225669 seen immediately after completion in October 1938. One of over 12,000 wagons to Diagram 63 without bottom doors, this one came from a batch numbered between 222972 to 225671 built in 1938. Several of these were the subject of conversions during the war, see plates 195 and 217. (BR)

PREFACE

In the 1970s the original Oxford Publishing Company included on its lists a series of authoritative illustrated works on a wide range of railway locomotives and rolling stock. The second of those on wagons, after the late Jim Russell's *A pictorial record of Great Western wagons*, was my own first book on the wagons of the LNER Company and its constituents. I know from the comments received since and the number of kits for modellers produced that this work met a need. Despite two further reprints, it has now been out of print for nearly a decade and a half and second hand copies are much sought after. It was with pleasure therefore that I accepted Pendragon's offer to reprint this again and I trust it will give the same satisfaction to readers and encourage them to model the subject matter described herein.

Apart from the first and last few pages, the content is exactly the same as the earlier editions, with the addition of a small erratum and addendum. It therefore falls to me to repeat my recognition of the support and assistance given by fellow members of the LNER Study Group both during the preparation of the original manuscript and since. Again the book is dedicated to them all, while those who provided specific help are mentioned in the acknowledgements at the end. Even so, it fell to me alone in this case to write the book and hence the final responsibility for all that goes with it must be mine.

From near the end of World War 1 in an effort to eliminate excessive empty mileage in returning wagons to their home territory, all ordinary open goods, coal and mineral wagons, together with non-fitted covered goods vans, which at the time represented the vast majority of freight stock in Great Britain, were pooled and operated on a common user basis. After grouping in 1923 this meant that each of the four railways contributed to the construction and maintenance of a common pool of such vehicles in proportion to the freight it carried. It was then at liberty to load and despatch any common user vehicle regardless of its ownership and of course the other companies were doing likewise. In general terms the effect was to mix all railway owned wagons and to spread them throughout the country in roughly the proportions of the four groups' total stock, with perhaps just a small bias to the home company. As the second largest of the four in this respect with approximately 38%, the London and North Eastern Railway deserves more than passing attention from all those seriously interested in the railway scene during that period, whatever their allegiance in locomotive and other matters.

It is the intention in the following pages to give an overview of the wagons used by the LNER and to study by means of the photographs and line drawings included, not only the standard designs built between 1923 and 1947, but a small sample of the vast range of wagons taken over from its six constituent companies. Also, because they do not readily fall into any other group, a few pages have been devoted to steam and hand travelling cranes. As a bridge engineer, who spent the first ten years of this career on the railways and many Saturday nights working with steam breakdown cranes, I could hardly leave them out.

An attempt has been made to portray a fair and balanced selection of vehicles of various origins wherever possible. Unlike the previous author, Jim Russell, I am not old enough to have photographed wagons in LNER days and have therefore had to rely on other sources. Many are official views and I suspect readers will soon notice how a certain white-washed wall at Doncaster tends to get more tatty as the years go by. To make a change and to add variety, photographs from several private collections have been included and these are especially useful in that they often depict the vehicles in other than pristine new conditions and frequently under traffic. Let me apologise in advance for a strong leaning to the Great Northern Railway's wagons and, conversely, a tendency to be a little light on Scottish vehicles. This was solely due to the availability of material at the time from which to compile this book and in no ways reflects a bias on my part: indeed if anything, the reverse is the case. For similar reasons, certain photographs have been included because of their interest, and in an effort to provide a proper balance in subject matter when not of top quality, it is hoped readers will still find these worthwhile.

It is over twenty years since this book was written and, although certain members of the LNER Study Group had been researching wagons for many years previous and special efforts were made at the time to unearth information likely to be of interest, a point was reached where one has to do the best with material then available. Nonetheless, from time to time fresh material does come to hand and we shall be pleased to hear from anyone with constructive criticism and additional information.

One suspects that a large percentage of railway enthusiasts have at some time or other built models of their idols and for this reason the line drawings have been reproduced to one of the common modelling scales — 4mm to 1 foot. I know a large number of kits and models have already been produced based on examples taken from this book and, as a modeller myself, if I have persuaded a few more readers to construct models of LNER wagons, then I shall feel that the reprint of this book has been worthwhile.

Peter Tatlow   February 1998

INTRODUCTION

PREGROUPING STOCK

When on 1st January 1923 the London North Eastern Railway was set up, it inherited the assets of the North Eastern (NER) including the Hull & Barnsley (H & B) absorbed during the previous year: the Great Northern (GN); Great Central (GC); Great Eastern (GE); North British (NB) and the Great North of Scotland (GNS) railways. The types and quantities of freight vehicles owned by these companies are listed in Appendix 1. Each railway had individual ideas on the design and long established practices in the construction of wagons and all had one or more workshops capable of supplying and maintaining most of the company's stock. The NER had several workshops, including those at Faverdale and Shildon which for wagon building purposes were collectively known as Darlington, while some construction was also undertaken at Heaton and York. The GN works were at the 'Plant', Doncaster; the GC at Dukinfield outside Manchester; the GE at Temple Mills in London, the NB at Cowlairs, Glasgow and the GNS, although a small railway, had a modern works at Inverurie, a little way north of Aberdeen.

The products of these wagon works showed considerable variety in both design and age; whilst some would be represented by only a few examples, others were to be found in large numbers. Capacity had been steadily increasing from 6 or 8 tons around the turn of the century to 10 tons for vans and 12 tons for open wagons, while experiments had been made in higher capacities and bogie vehicles. Automatic vacuum and Westinghouse brakes were in use for some freight stock, but by 1923 were fitted only to 9,600 vehicles and these were usually employed for special traffics requiring rapid transit. During the period under consideration from 1923 to 1947, the older and small wagons were withdrawn, although many of the more numerous recent pregrouping designs survived the whole of this period in quantity and lasted some while with British Railways. An idea of the survival rate may be gained from Appendix 2 showing the numbers of pregrouping stock remaining during the later years of the LNER. At grouping many small subsidiary companies were absorbed by the LNER of which the following three owned rolling stock, the Colne Valley and Halstead Railway 174 wagons, East and West Yorkshire Union Railway 201 and Mid-Suffolk Light Railways 21.

As part owners of two joint railways, the LNER shared with the LMS the Cheshire Lines Committee (CLC) and the Midland and Great Northern Joint Railway (M & GN). Prior to 1923 the former was the property of the GN, GC and Midland Railways and therefore two-thirds fell to the LNER and one-third to the LMS, whilst the M & GN was shared equally by the two partners. Both joint companies possessed their own stock, but it was soon decided to make

the parent companies responsible for the provision of wagons for traffic purposes and the existing stock was shared out between them in the above proportions. In this way the LNER took over the following:-

Joint Company	CLC	M&GN
Date taken over	1/1/30	1/10/36
Open wagons	1936	55
Covered goods vans	551	23
Refrigerator & meat vans	27	-
Bolster wagons	108	11
Cattle trucks	104	68
Specially constructed vehicles	14	2
Total:	2740	160

Brake vans and service vehicles were retained by the joint companies for the time being.

Plate 1

LNER STANDARD DESIGNS

In 1923 the Railway Clearing House (RCH) issued a new specification for a 12 ton mineral wagon. To a greater or lesser degree the four main railway companies adopted many of its features and component parts for use in their own designs and in view of the common user scheme then in operation, this probably had much to commend it from the point of view of availability of spare parts at outlying repair depots. The usual capacity for both wagons and vans

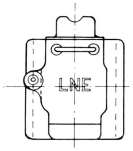
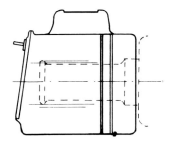

Figure 1

Figure 2

from now on was 12 tons and for nearly a decade the wheelbase was 9 feet. The latter can only be regarded as a retrograde step when it is borne in mind that several companies had been using 10 feet or 10 ft. 6 in. immediately prior to grouping and since subsequently the standard was changed back to 10 ft. in about 1932.

Initially almost all the RCH fittings were used by the LNER on stock not fitted with automatic brakes and indeed 12 ton mineral wagons, gunpowder vans and containers were built straight from RCH drawings. A noticeable feature of both LNER and LMS wagons at this time was the extensive use of timber underframes and it can in part be ascribed to previous heavy investment in workshops laid out and equipped to produce this type in large quantities. A timber frame being lowered onto the wheels and running gear by some of this equipment can be seen in plate 1. The majority of open and mineral wagons and vans had wooden underframes until 1936 in the case of vans, although fish vans continued thus for sometime, and up to 1948 for 13 ton hopper wagons; whilst the LNER never built a cattle truck with anything else but timber underframes.

The RCH design of cast iron split axle box was employed at first, but from about 1932 was replaced by the cast steel open fronted type shown in figure 1. This subsequently was developed into an all welded one with a pressed steel front, mass production of these being undertaken at Shildon from 1939. Changes in buffer housings and wheels can be seen over the years and not always with any consistency. Some buffer housings had very small fillets at the sides only, while on others three webs ran from the base to the outer end with the fourth on top stopped short to form a notch in which the shunter could rest his pole for raising the

coupling, see figure 2. Spoked wheels were supplied on early batches of wagons, but from 1934 three hole disc became the rule, except when reprofiled second-hand spoked wheels were fitted to new stock. Later on, of course, it was not unknown for one of each type to be under the one vehicle.

During the interwar period the LNER's wagon building programme was severely hampered by the economic straits of both the Company and Britain as a whole, until rearmament programmes took effect from 1936. However, it set about the construction of modern stock to replace the older pregrouping wagons with increasing emphasis being put on the provision of automatic vacuum brakes on vehicles for use in express freight trains, together with the introduction of containers. Appendix 3 shows the total stock of the Company for the years 1929, 1938 and 1947.

AUTOMATIC VACUUM BRAKE GEAR

Prior to grouping the automatic vacuum brake (AVB) was used by all the constituent companies except for two major ones, the NE and GE, together with the GNS which employed the Westinghouse compressed air brake, while the NB was currently using both having already decided to convert from Westinghouse to vacuum. In addition, some vehicles were fitted with a through pipe and connecting hoses for the alternative system and occasionally fully dual fitted for both types. However, despite the prevalence of the Westinghouse system the LNER decided, in common with the others of the 'Big Four', to standardise on the vacuum brake for all new construction.

Plate 2

Plate 3

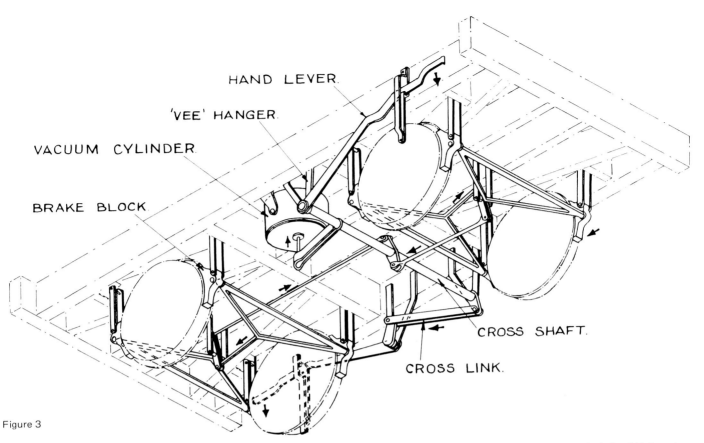

HAND LEVER.

'VEE' HANGER.

VACUUM CYLINDER.

BRAKE BLOCK.

CROSS SHAFT.

CROSS LINK.

Figure 3

The means by which the action of applying the brakes by vacuum brake cylinder to a compensated brake, and also making it possible to operate them by hand levers from either side of the vehicle, is perhaps difficult to put across, especially when none of the other companies used a similar design. At first sight it appears that under the solebar there is a host of rods and levers, each hung from the previous bit. The mechanism used by the LNER actually originated on the GN and basically consists of three 'V' hangers, two on one side equally disposed about the centre of the vehicle when viewed in elevation and the third on the opposite side and in line with one on the first side and between which a cross shaft is fitted, see figure 3 and plate 2. Operating directly on this shaft is one hand lever and the vacuum cylinder. Because it is on the opposite side, the direction of rotation of the second lever has to be reversed before being applied to the shaft and the cross link between the two 'V' hangers on that side performs this function. The pull to the brakes is taken from each end of a double lever attached to the shaft at the longitudinal centre line of the vehicle. The braking force is applied twice to all four wheels across their horizontal diameter, thus eight brake blocks are brought into play. To ensure even pressure on all of them the elaborate system of suspended links and cross yokes is required, these are further detailed in figure 4 and plate 3.

This arrangement was used for all standard fitted LNER vehicles with both timber and steel underframes. Variations in wheel base were catered for by increasing the length of the cross link, while maintaining the 'V' hangers at three feet from the adjacent axle in all cases. Screw couplings

instead of the ordinary three link and 1 ft. 8½ ins. long buffers as opposed to the normal 1 ft. 6 ins. were always used on fitted stock.

DIAGRAM BOOKS

All of the constituent companies had a book of diagrams, each diagram showing in outline the basic shape and dimensions of every individual design owned by that company. In the case of the larger companies the book might amount to over two hundred diagrams and the NER issued a book for specially constructed vehicles as well. In addition, the GN produced a rather fine book entitled *'Illustrations of Wagon Stock'*. As and when new stock was built, existing altered or the last vehicle withdrawn amendment slips would be issued to keep the books up to date.

Initially it seems each pregrouping company's diagram book was perpetuated, although the titles were changed for example to LNE-C, LNE-SSA, LNE-NSA for the ex.GC, NB and GNS books respectively, and diagrams of standard LNER vehicles were added to these as addendums. A *'List of Diagrams of London & North Eastern Railway Specially Constructed Wagons'* was issued by the Central Wagon Control Office at York in 1926 and included all pregrouping stock of this description. An LNER book of standard wagons does not appear to have arrived on the scene much before 1929 and as well as including specially constructed vehicles built since 1923, had some ordinary vehicles of pregrouping origins probably built in the few years immediately after grouping. Over the years this book was added to until it amounted to a total of 227 diagrams,

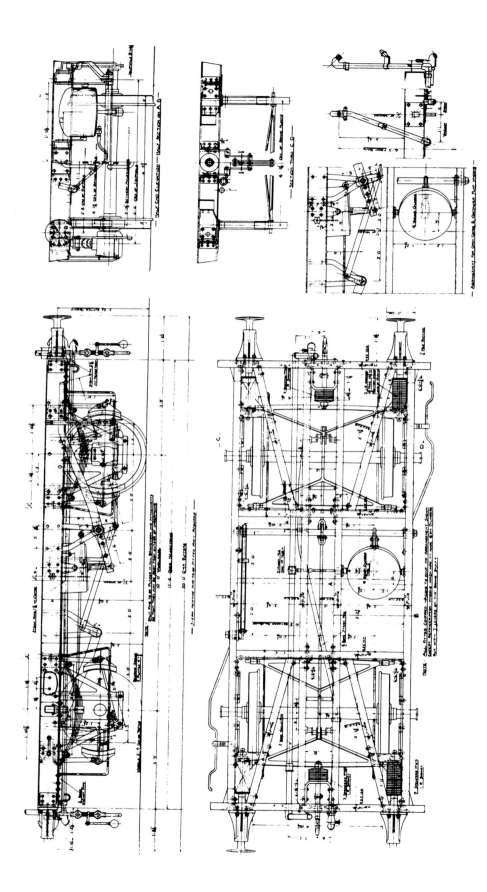

ARRANGEMENT OF VACUUM BRAKEGEAR ON WAGON UNDERFRAME.

Figure 4

4

although the last few are for wagons built after the LNER's demise. The quality and amount of detail included on these and some pregrouping diagrams is quite high and many will be found reproduced in the following pages.

WAGON CODES

To enable a concise and accurate description of each type of wagon to be conveyed particularly in a message by telegraph, all wagons were allocated a code. Initially this was in the form of a short word, often actually indicating its purpose, and could cover vehicles of several different diagrams. It could be suffixed by a letter to distinguish between types and this was particularly done with specially constructed stock, where of course there was a greater need to be definite in the exact type of vehicle referred to. The word codes used are listed in Appendix 4.

In 1938 a system of automated wagon control was introduced, not that a computer as we know it today was used, but a system of punched cards was instituted and under this arrangement each type of wagon was referred to by digit code which was in fact, its diagram number. LNER standard diagrams retained their numbers, while remaining diagrams for pregrouping stock were renumbered with four digits, where the first indicated the company of origin thus:-

ex GN	4001 to 4128
ex GC and CLC	5001 to 5326
ex GE	6001 to 6066
ex NB	7001 to 7146
ex GNS	8001 to 8042
ex NER	9001 to 9182
ex H & B	9901 to 9927

NUMBERING

Each constituent company had its own wagon numbering scheme which, for the most part, consisted of reusing numbers as they became vacant, before adding further numbers to the end of the list. Because withdrawals occurred as and when the older vehicles became life expired or beyond repair following accident damage, the numbers were reused in a totally random way. This may have been convenient to the companies concerned, if all that was required was a reasonable idea of the total number of their stock; but it is highly confusing to the historian, to whom the issue of a block of numbers for each batch of newly constructed wagons, makes his studies a great deal easier.

Before going on to describe how the LNER integrated the various numbering systems, a word on the North Eastern Railway's practice in wagon numbering in the period immediately prior to 1923 is called for. The NER, as owners of the largest wagon fleet in Britain, was faced with the prospect of having to employ six digits as its numbers grew and adopted a unique solution to the problem in an effort to make the wagon checker's task easier and less prone to error. From about 1908 use was made of only three digits and a prefix letter and this was continued up to 1922, when Z would have been reached. The thought of double letters and three digits was too much to bear and a return to six

digits was decided upon and the numbers 110001 to 129000 were allotted, although it was some time into the postgrouping era before the renumbering was actually applied to all the wagons. It should be noted that the letters H, I, O, P, Q and X were not used, partly because of the likelihood of their being misread for numerals. The Hull and Barnsley Railway, which was absorbed by the NER in April 1922, simply had 'HB' added as a prefix to their wagon numbers and for some reason this was not thereafter altered.

In view of the fact that the NER had the most numerous stock of wagons, the LNER left their numbers alone, except for completing the replacement of letters by larger numerals, and made up all the other companies numbers to six digits, by adding to them the following:-

GN	400000
GC	500000
GE	600000
NB	700000
GNS	800000

The intention then seems to have been to expand upon the NER series, including initially until 1929 using up numbers falling vacant due to withdrawals. The first vehicles built for the LNER were of course to pregrouping designs and a little confusion ensued when some were numbered with their appropriate pregrouping companies stock and others in the ex. NER list, but the latter were subsequently renumbered if they were to a pregrouping diagram.

Although from 1929 the LNER gave up trying to fill vacant spots in the existing list and numbered sequentially, it never settled down to use blocks of numbers for specific batches of any particular design until near the end of its existence, except when wagons were built by outside contractors. In the Darlington complex, wagons arrived at Faverdale for painting from the several Works in the vicinity and, if various types were put together in the line, that is the order in which they were numbered. From 1929 there was a little more order to the chaos, but the Company still thought nothing of numbering brake fitted and nonfitted or five and six plank opens in the same series, and therefore for the most part it has not proved possible to give readers blocks of numbers for the various designs of vehicles to be described in the following pages.

Most of the constituent companies seem to have gone in for rectangular cast iron number plates and plate 4 shows a GN example found on an Engineer's vehicle at York as late as June 1972. Those of the NER, H & B, NB and M & GN Jt. had scalloped corners, while the NER used serif style numerals. Because no renumbering was involved the NER and H & B plates were generally retained by the LNER, whereas all the others were replaced by the RCH standard 10 x 6 inch plate with rounded bottom. In the case of renumbered pregrouping stock the ownership was stated on some plates as LNER — plus a letter indicating its origin as follows:-

D — ex NE
N — ex GN
C — ex GC
E — ex GE
B — ex NB etc.

It is not always wise to place too much reliance on the statements made on builders' plates. Once when measuring up a 'Toad E' brake van it was noticed that while the plates on each side could agree on the number and year of construction, one proclaimed that the van was built at Doncaster, the other side said Darlington. One could only conclude that the two halves were assembled into one unit at York!

Several of the constituent companies used a separate series when numbering service stock and for a few years following grouping this practice was continued. However, by the early thirties some vehicles at least were being numbered into the following series according to the former constituent companies territories to which they were allocated, viz:-

20xxxx	North Eastern Area	
47xxxx	Southern Area,	GN Section
54xxxx		GC Section
63xxxx		GE Section
77xxxx	Southern Scottish Area	
88xxxx	Northern Scottish Area	

Nonetheless, nothing daunted, a new scheme was devised for departmental stock in 1938 and introduced the following year. Under this six digits were used again, but '9' was always the first figure, the second indicating the area to which the vehicle belonged, thus:-

90xxxx	North Eastern Area	
94xxxx	Southern Area — GN Section	
95xxxx		GC Section
96xxxx		GE Section
97xxxx	Southern Scottish Area	
98xxxx	Northern Scottish Area	

The third digit was used to denote the department operating the wagon, the Engineers being 'O', Locomotive Department '1', the Workshops '2' and Stores '3'. Should a wagon be transferred from revenue earning stock or transferred from one area to another, it would have been renumbered into the recipient's list and is therefore no indication of its origin.

Plate 4

PREGROUPING LIVERIES

Although a standard painting scheme was issued and in use by June 1924, the ordinary humble wagon was not repainted as frequently as the locomotive or coach and wagons still in pregrouping livery were to be found as late as 1938, even if they were by then looking decidedly dog-eared. So brief details of pregrouping liveries are given below for the period immediately prior to 1923:-

North Eastern   Grey bodywork with white lettering and black undergear, some brake vans in red oxide. Mineral wagons carried letters ND, CD or SD indicating that the vehicle was allocated to Northern, Central or Southern Divisions of the system.

Hull and Barnsley   Bodywork dark blue or lead grey and white letters.

Great Northern   Brown red oxide with white lettering and black undergear. Refrigerator and meat vans were white with black lettering, while gunpowder vans were also white but with red lettering.

Great Central   Lead grey bodywork with white lettering and black running gear. Refrigerator vans were in a lighter shade of grey with black shading to the white letters of 'GC', while 'Refrigerator' was in red. The GC was fond of long inscriptions in raised cast iron letters picked out in white on black boards screwed to the body sides.

Great Eastern   Dark grey bodywork with white lettering, black below the solebar. Vermillion headstocks to brake vans.

North British   Grey bodywork sometimes with the ironwork picked out in black, lettering white. Running gear, buffers and draw gear in black. An inverted crescent painted on the wagon sides contained two figures which indicated the year of construction or the last general overhaul. The company's vehicles also carried a small quatrefoil, thought to be an easily recognisable symbol for the illiterate railwayman. Service vehicles, gunpowder vans and some brake vans were red oxide in colour.

Great Northern of Scotland   Dark grey woodwork with black ironwork and white lettering. Service stock had dark red instead of grey woodwork.

Cheshire Lines Committee   Bodywork pale lead grey, black running gear and white lettering.

Midland & Gt. Northern Joint   Dark grey bodies with white lettering.

10 TON REFRIGERATOR VAN   DIAGRAM. F10

LETTERS 4" ← NON ... 1ST REFRIGERATOR

N   E

LETTERS 18×12"
FIGURES 5"

3½ FIGURES

1½ FIGURES

Figure 5

LNER LIVERY

The LNER standardised the colour of its freight stock for the whole of its existence as follows:-

Bodywork -
- Grey for nonfitted wagons and covered vans in revenue earning service, together with loco coal and sleeper wagons, but excluding brake vans.
- Brown red oxide for all vehicles fitted with automatic brake and also all brake vans. Although the specification for this colour was changed to bauxite around 1940, the appearance seems to have remained much the same.
- White on refrigerator vans with black ladders, footboards and sometimes parts of the strapping and door latches.
- Oxford blue for service vehicles, such as engineers and stores wagons.
- Green for vehicles restricted to yard or limited trip use.
- Black on breakdown cranes with ¼ inch red lining, also some loco coal and service wagons were painted this colour, mostly during wartime.

The bodywork was deemed to include the solebars and headstocks if of timber, but steel underframes were painted black.

Van Roofs - White lead, the colour of roof vents could be either white as well or black. Some roofs seem to have been painted grey at the outset rather than waiting for an accumulated layer of grime and smuts to turn them that colour. Later the roofs of fitted vans were bauxite like the bodywork.

Running Gear - Black on all wheels, axles, brake fittings, buffers and draw gear. The ends of brake levers were painted white to make them easier to see in poor light conditions. Whether wheel rims were picked out in white as a general rule rather than the odd few just to have their official photograph taken seems uncertain.

The shades of these colours, even when straight out of the paint shop, were not always the same. Comparison between the product of the various railway and contractor's works could show marked differences. To the railways paint on freight stock was simply a protection against the elements and an exact match in colour was simply not important to them: indeed from about 1943 they even gave up painting the woodwork of open and mineral wagons and painted all metalwork black. Due to the action of weathering and bleaching by sunlight over the years between repaints must be added varying amounts of dirt from the traffic carried and the industrial surroundings most vehicles found themselves in for the majority of their lives. White was hardly likely to stay that way for long, while the red oxide would tend to change colour over the years. Blue is notoriously unstable and service vehicles are often described as dark or pale blue, as if they were either from Oxford or Cambridge: but, although a variety of hues were undoubtedly applied, it is much more likely that they gradually changed from one to the other with ever increasing exposure to the elements. The vacuum train pipes of vehicles fitted with automatic brakes were painted black, whereas those that only had through pipes had the pipes painted red.

The first style of lettering indicated the wagon's ownership by just the middle two letters 'NE', generally in the large size of 18 by 12 inches either side of the door on the more usual types of vehicles, but these could be reduced in size as necessary on low sided vehicles. The running number was underneath the 'E' in 5 inch numerals on the right hand side, except vans with sliding doors which had the numbers on the doors. The vehicle code (if any, see Appendix 4) was above the capacity both being in 4 inch letters on the left hand side as laid out in figure 5 of an ex. NER ventilated refrigerated van. The tare weight was generally written in 3½ inch figures on the solebar just inside the right hand wheel. The month and year that the wagon was painted (P) and lifted off its wheels (L) was stencilled in 1¼ inch figures above this, while on the solebar above the right hand wheel a 12 inch wide patch was painted, upon which the 'date oiled' and 'District No.' could be chalked. These words were stencilled on from December 1930, leaving just the actual date to be entered in chalk. The colour of the patch was black on a grey background and dark grey on red oxide or black. Automatic brake fitted wagons had the position of the vacuum release cord indicated by a six pointed star attached to the solebar, while Westinghouse equipped had the letter 'W'.

Figure 6

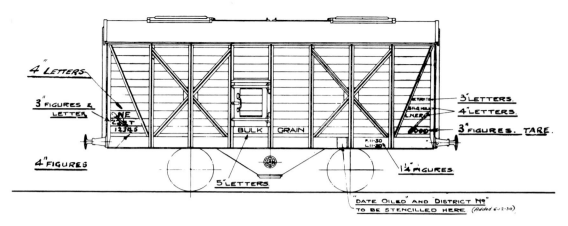

POSITION OF LETTERING ETC, ON 20 TON BULK GRAIN WAGON (NON-CONVERTIBLE TYPE)

WAGONS TO BE PAINTED AS FOLLOWS:-

UNDERFRAME:- WHEELS & AXLES, BRAKE GEAR, UNDERFRAMES & ALL OTHER UNDERFRAME IRONWORK
TO BE:- BLACK.
HOPPER TO BE:- BLACK.

BODY & BODY IRONWORK:- GREY.

ALL WRITING ON ABOVE TO BE WHITE.

:-CHALK DATE TO BE PAINTED GREY.

Automatic brake fitted wagons also had the wheel base stated on the right hand end of the solebar. Lettering was in white, except on the bodywork of refrigerated vans when it was black.

From about 1926 non-common user vehicles were singled out by painting the letter 'N' 4 inches high in the two bottom corners of the bodywork or on the ends of the headstocks. In the early '30s the wagon code was moved to the middle of the body, usually onto the door. About this time also the cast iron code plate was introduced for fruit and fish vans as depicted in plate 5. In 1936 the number came over to the left hand side and the tare weight took its place. This may have been an experiment prior to the next and more radical change about to be made. Certainly it was not in vogue for long and therefore not many wagons received it.

In common with the other post grouping companies, the LNER adopted a revised layout of lettering for new and re-painted stock from 1937. The Company initials 'NE' were reduced in size to 4 inch, placed over the capacity in 3 inch, which in turn was above the running number in 4 inch: all to the bottom left hand corner with 3 inch spaces between lines, although this might be modified to avoid joints in the planking. The tare weight was shown in 3 inch letters on the bottom right hand corner; for a short while this was quoted in tons, cwt and qtrs, but soon reverted to just the first two. The revised lettering layout is illustrated in figure 6 of a non-convertible bulk grain hopper.

In plate 6, due to the weathering away of some of the latter layers of paint, it is possible to demonstrate the position of the different lettering schemes on the same wagon. The large letters 'N' and 'E' are readily apparent with the number on the right hand side. But on the left hand side the whole thing is repeated with the smaller size of Company initials. When photographed this ex. GN 10 ton six plank open wagon was reaching the end of its working life and restricted to West Hartlepool Docks only, hence the two vertical white stripes at the left hand end.

A year or so after the introduction of the small lettered livery, the wheel base dimension was moved to above the tare weight on automatic brake fitted vehicles and if more than 10 feet, the letters 'XP' were applied in 4 inch letters above the 'WB'. During the war each of the letter sizes to this livery was reduced by an inch as an economy measure. Because of the protracted period between repaints and the fact that during the war this was even further extended by patch painting, many wagons were still to be seen running with the large letters well after the war. In 1945 the 'P' and 'L' dates were moved to the right hand end of the solebar.

Plate 6

Plate 7

The open wagon with full length dropsides of two, three or even four planks was a common vehicle on the pregrouping railways, and all the LNER constituents contributed some of one sort or another to the Company's stock. It therefore had sufficient for its needs and found it unnecessary to build any to its own design. They were used to convey a wide variety of goods and in latter days often employed as service vehicles.

In plate 7 a GN 9 ton dropside built at Doncaster in 1904, can be seen resplendent in its new LNER livery. Note the rings on the solebar and headstocks used when tying down tarpaulin wagon sheets or securing a load. The brakes are unusual with each side lever of opposite hand and brake blocks acting on the left hand wheel both sides. Figure 7 is a diagram of this type of vehicle which was built in 8, 9 and 10 ton versions and known as 'Colwick' wagons.

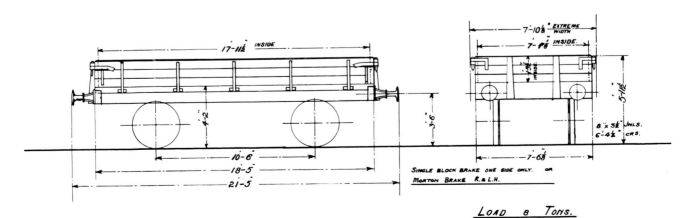

Figure 7

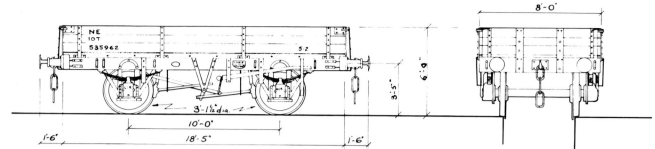

Figure 8

Figure 8 shows a GC 10 ton 3 plank dropside. It has two wheel braking, but the two levers are right handed and the nearer is reversed by acting through a fulcrum onto a short lever from the 'V' hanger. Plate 8 is of a NER 12 ton plank dropside built in 1920.

In the days when covered wagons or vans were very much in the minority, tarpaulin wagon sheets were frequently used to protect loads likely to be damaged by inclement weather or engine sparks. Figure 9 is one in LNER lettering, the tarpaulin would be black with white lettering. Note the date of manufacture indicated by the month over the year, i.e. 5/1925. The layout of the lettering was later simplified with the letters 'LNE' over the number at each end only.

Figure 9

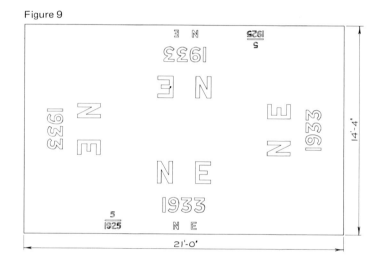

Plate 8

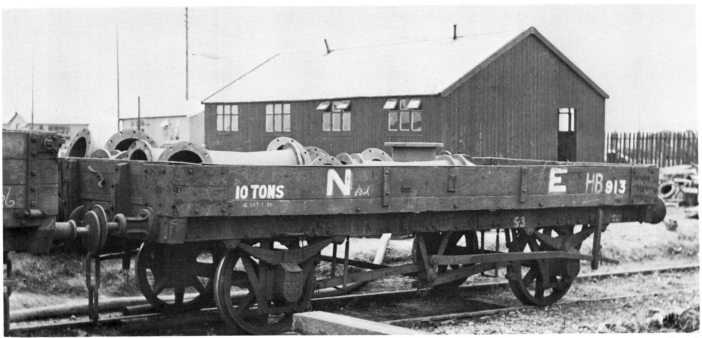

Plate 9

Plate 10

A number of the constituent pregrouping companies had low fixed sided wagons usually of only one plank in height. The first in plate 9 is a Hull and Barnsley 10 ton example seen at Cardington in May 1939 loaded with some special pipe fittings. Next in plate 10 is a somewhat shorter NB 8 ton pig iron wagon put out to grass after the war with other ancient vehicles and no doubt waiting to be broken up. Plate 11 shows a GNS 8 ton three plank at Plaistow (LT & S) around 1937 being used as a locomotive coal wagon. Note the larger diameter wheels, also that all three vehicles are fitted with grease lubricated axle boxes and both wagons of Scottish origin have the company initials and number painted on the solebar as well as on the bodywork and carrying builders' plates.

Plate 11

Plate 12

Plate 13

8 TON OPEN WAGONS

The more usual form of open wagon had doors in the middle of each side, as shown in the following pages. Plate 12 is of a GN 3 plank with radiused ends and pole at the highest point on the longitudinal centre line of the wagon. This would be used to support a wagon sheet thus forming a crude tent over the load. The brake gear is similar to that in plate 7, but is viewed from the other side with the brake lever to the left hand end.

Turning north of the border to Scotland for the origins of plates 13 and 14, photographed in the late '30s, in the first we have a NB 4 plank with simple lever and push rod acting on one brake shoe. Another, but unconnected set is fitted on the other side. Plate 14 is the GNS 3 plank version at Plaistow; however, because the planks are wider the height of the side is about the same.

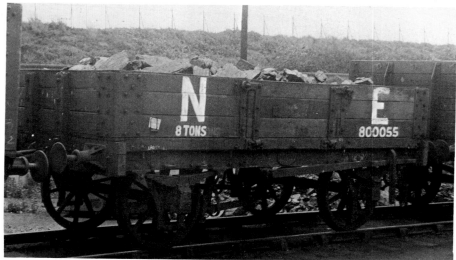

Plate 14

The Great Northern's 9 ton 4 plank open was extremely common, the LNER taking over 11,664 of them, although admittedly their numbers were to drop drastically by the beginning of the War, so that 396 remained by the end of 1941 and only 28 were passed on to British Railways at nationalisation. Figure 10 and plate 15, photographed at Cricklewood, are of the version with wooden underframes, but there were some on steel underframes as illustrated in plate 16 of which the LNER received 590. The axle boxes, again grease lubricated, and the buffer housings, are typical hall-marks of their GN origins. A small cast iron plate to the bottom left hand corner of the bodywork says 'Load 10 tons distributed'.

Plate 15

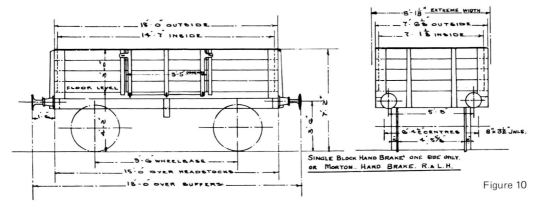

Figure 10

Plate 16

NER AND H & B 10 TON OPEN WAGONS

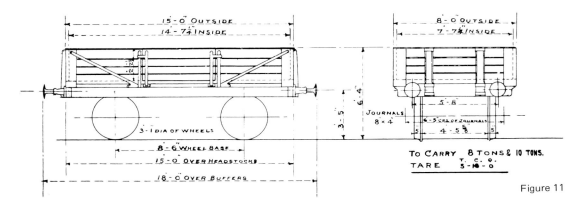

Figure 11

The NER 4 plank open wagon to figure 11 started life with a capacity of 8 tons, but from 1904 8 in. by 4 in. size journals were fitted in place of 8 in. by 3½ in. and the load plates altered to read 10 tons distributed load.

Two types of Hull and Barnsley 10 ton open wagons are depicted in plate 17 and figure 12. The photograph taken on 26 July 1939 is a wagon 15 ft. 6 in. over headstock of four planks and with grease axleboxes. Note the extremely simple braking, the hidden diagonal bracing to the ends, the wooden door stop bolted to the solebar and that the HB number and number plate have been retained. Although this wagon has been lettered in the post '37 style, the patches over the previous lettering are apparent.

A more recent H & B design for a 10 ton open 18 ft. 6 in. long over headstocks and of five planks is the diagram reproduced as figure 12.

Plate 17

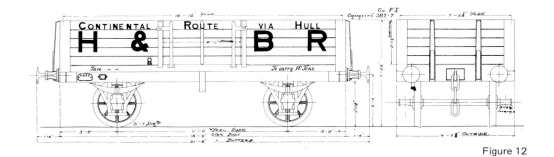

Figure 12

GN 10 TON 6 PLANK OPEN WAGON

Plate 18

Plate 19

The GN 10 ton six plank open wagons 19 feet over the headstocks were built in both automatic vacuum brake fitted and unfitted versions, although the latter as illustrated in plate 18 predominated. Close up details of the spring, 'W' iron and oil lubricated axle box are shown in plate 20 while plate 21 is of the brake 'V' hanger, reversing clutch of the 'Moreton' type brake, flitched solebar and door spring.

A few wagons had frames fixed above the sides so that they could be used for the conveyance of vegetables, as can be seen in plate 19. The vehicle had through pipe to maintain the continuity of the automatic vacuum brake along the train, but is not itself equipped with anything more than a hand brake. The letter 'N' at each bottom corner of the bodywork indicated that the wagon did not come under the common user arrangement.

Plate 20

Plate 21

Plate 22

Plate 23

Plate 24

GE 10 TON 5 PLANK OPEN WAGONS

Steel underframes were a common feature of much Great Eastern freight stock, as is clearly seen in these views of 10 ton open wagons 15 feet over the headstocks. Plate 22 is of a wagon built in 1901 in the early style of livery: photographed at Kings Lynn around 1937, and appears to be carrying loco coal. In plate 23 a recently painted vehicle at Cardington in May 1938 has the new scheme of lettering. Note the ratchet teeth used to hold down the brake lever instead of the more usual series of holes through which a pin was inserted. Two varieties of buffer housings have been fitted to the one vehicle in the case of this wagon and that depicted in plates 25 and 26. The typical design of GE axle boxes is shown in plate 24.

Plate 25

An increase in size, but not load carrying capacity, was obtained in the 17 foot long seven plank open shown in figure 13 and plates 24 to 26 of No. 606437 built in 1910. Although at first sight this type resembles a mineral wagon, by the provision of two side hung top doors, there is an opening for loading for the full depth of the sides and it is therefore classed as an open wagon. Versions of this design were fitted with tarpaulin rails for sheeted loads. As well as the unusual arrangement of the door, the double diagonal bracing and patent door-stop should be noticed.

Plate 26

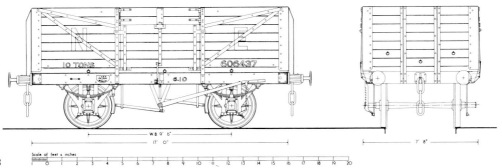

Figure 13

Plate 27

During World War 1 the railway companies supplied vast quantities of manufactured goods for the war effort in the form of both military and railway equipment. As well as locomotives and ambulance trains, wagons were required in their thousands and plate 27 shows a 10 ton six plank open wagon on a steel underframe of GC design built by that company for the War Department. For use on the Continent it has been fitted with screw couplings and extended buffers: similar wagons without these latter features were owned by the Company.

The last design of the NER for an open wagon was of 12 tons capacity and had six planks as shown in plates 28 and 29. In the first the wagon is 'as built' by Hurst Nelson in 1920 and is painted in the NER's livery. Note the smaller size of letters 'NE' and the prefixed number. The second depicts a similar wagon in LNER days.

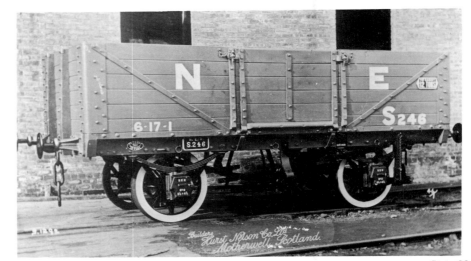

Plate 28

Plate 29

Plate 30

We now come to the LNER's first standard design and undoubtedly the most prolific of them all, although as we shall see there were variations. Actually, the drawings for the initial batch were prepared by the GN at Doncaster in June 1921 and 100 were constructed prior to grouping. Many standard RCH components such as buffers, axle boxes and guard irons and brake fittings were incorporated on the wooden underframe of 9 foot wheel base. Construction continued at both Doncaster and Darlington, and elsewhere, until there was a total of over 20,000. Plate 30 shows the Darlington version and the long taper to the steel tee section end stanchions, together with the wheels, should be compared with the Doncaster product in plate 32.

Six plank open wagons of 9 foot wheelbase were produced with automatic vacuum brake gear, but in the earlier years of the LNER there was not a very great demand for such wagons and only a few hundred were constructed. An example built in 1934 is shown in plate 31 and would have been painted red oxide, as opposed to the grey of the unfitted wagons.

Plate 31

Plate 32

LNER 12 TON 6 PLANK OPEN WAGONS

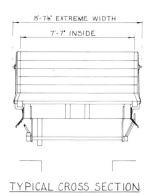

8'-7⅛" EXTREME WIDTH
7'-7" INSIDE

TYPICAL CROSS SECTION

Figure 14

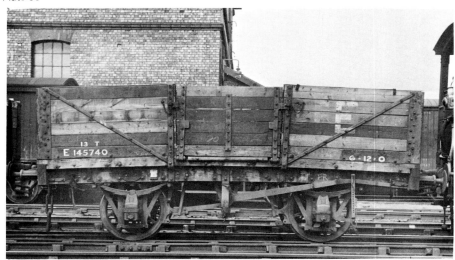

BRAKE GEAR ON FAR SIDE SHOWN DOTTED.

N E

12 TONS   43326

6·10

1'-6' 4'-3'   9'-0' WHEELBASE   4'-3' 1'-6'
17'-6' OVER HEADSTOCKS
3·5¼'

ELEVATION

WHEELS 3'-1⅛' DIA. 8 № SPOKES

8'-0' OVER BODY
1'-1' DIA
4'-1¼' TO FLOOR
7'-6¾'

END VIEW

Plate 33

13 T
E 145740   20   6·12·0

The 9 foot wheelbase timber under-frame of open wagons and other types, notably the cattle truck, seems to have had a weakness which caused some wagons to become 'hump backed', as plate 33 taken at Bedford in June 1952 amply demonstrates.

Figure 14 is a drawing of an open wagon with 9 foot wheelbase. However, from about 1932 this was increased to 10 feet and construction continued, as shown in plate 34 of No. 238879 built in 1940, until these numbered some 15,000. Subsequently they were made with hard-wood bodies and finally on steel under-frames.

Plate 34

N E
13 T
238879   6·16

103/1078/1

LNER 12 TON 6 PLANK OPEN WAGONS

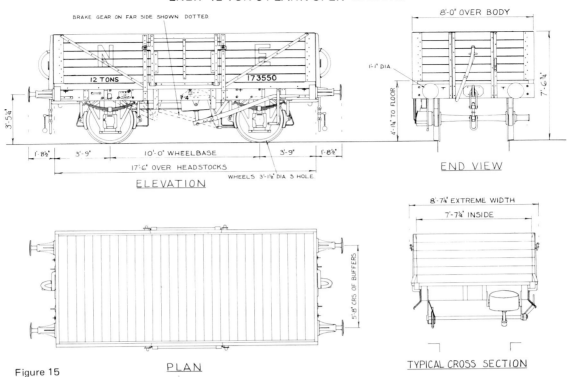

BRAKE GEAR ON FAR SIDE SHOWN DOTTED

N E

12 TONS   173550

3'-5¼"

1'-8½"   3'-9"   10'-0" WHEELBASE   3'-9"   1'-8½"

17'-6" OVER HEADSTOCKS

WHEELS 3'-1½" DIA 3 HOLE

ELEVATION

8'-0" OVER BODY

1'-1" DIA

4'-1¼" TO FLOOR

7'-6¼"

END VIEW

5'-8" CRS OF BUFFERS

PLAN

Figure 15

8'-7⅛" EXTREME WIDTH

7'-7¼" INSIDE

TYPICAL CROSS SECTION

Plate 35

The increase in wheelbase to 10 feet coincided with a greater need for AVB fitted open wagons and over 6,000 were built in a few years to the form shown in figure 15. Plate 35 is of one built in 1938 and has the cast steel open fronted axle boxes and three hole disc wheels as opposed to the split type of axle box and spoked wheels on earlier vehicles.

The final version of six plank open was provided at last with a steel underframe and hardwood body. The latter was no doubt thought to need no further treatment and therefore paint was only applied to the metal parts together with small patches upon which to place the lettering. Plate 36 shows an example built in 1945. The vertical members each side of the door are steel angle sections the foot of which is riveted to extension plates from the solebar.

Plate 36

LNER 12 TON 5 PLANK AND 13 TON 7 PLANK OPEN WAGONS

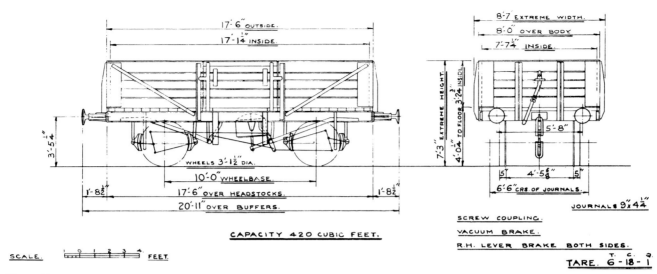

CAPACITY 420 CUBIC FEET.

SCREW COUPLING.
VACUUM BRAKE.
R.H. LEVER BRAKE BOTH SIDES.
TARE. 6-18-1

Figure 16

Plate 37

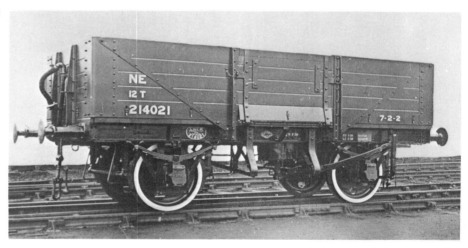

In 1938 the design of AVB fitted open wagons was revised to the one shown in figure 16 and plate 37 with five planks and steel underframe. No. 214021 in plate 37 was built in that year by R.Y. Pickering. For the conveyance of aircraft propellors 150 wagons of this type were converted, each being capable of carrying a pair of three blade air screws in crates. Later they reverted to open wagons.

The early war days found the LNER short of open wagons and in 1941 some 200 were hurriedly converted from surplus seven plank end door mineral wagons (see page 52) by the simple expedient of cutting out the top two planks over the door and increasing the height of the door by one plank as shown in plate 38 of No. 223259. The fact that these planks used to pass from one end of the vehicle to the other emphasizes the distinction between open and mineral types of wagon.

Plate 38

22

Plate 39

Plate 40

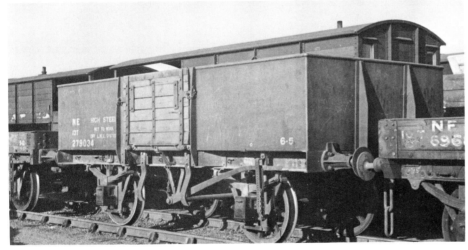

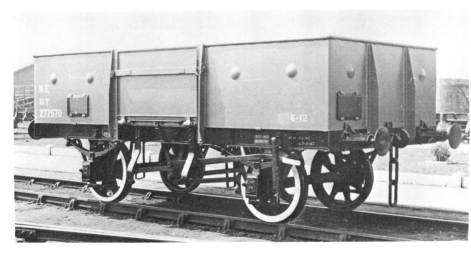

Having clung to the timber wagon under-frames for so long, the LNER then changed course drastically and started in 1945 to produce open wagons with steel bodies. The non-fitted version shown on this page was produced with both steel and six plank timber doors. The wagon pictured in plate 39 is incomplete, as the highlights on the running gear suggest that it has yet to receive its timber floor. The embossed builder's plate on the solebar is unusual. Plate 40 shows a similar wagon in traffic with the lettering completed. Below 'HIGH STEEL', it reads 'NOT TO WORK OFF LNE SYSTEM', so presumably at this time these vehicles were not part of the common user arrangement. Plate 41 is of the steel door model and has dimples in the body sides, to accommodate rings inside to which ropes securing loads may be tied. The boards mounted on the side to the left of the door and on the ends often indicated the yard to which the vehicles were to be returned when empty.
Numbers were:-

Steel door	277479 to 277578
Six Plank door	278709 to 279208

Plate 41

LNER 13 TON ALL STEEL HIGH SIDED OPEN WAGONS

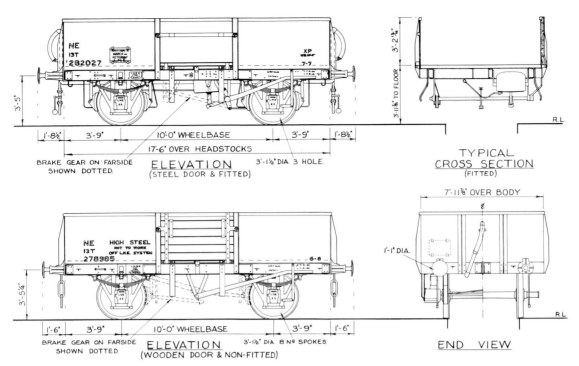

Figure 17

Figure 17 is a drawing of both AVB fitted and non-fitted versions of the all steel open wagons. Plate 42 illustrates another incomplete vehicle, this time fitted with AVB. It is thought that the underframes were built in railway workshops and that the fabrication of the steel bodywork was contracted out, in this case to the Teesside Bridge and

Engineering Works Ltd. of Middlesbrough and the floors added elsewhere. Substantial numbers of these vehicles were built, numbered 280209 to 283208 and 293145 to 296844. 3,562 were on the books at nationalisation, the second batch still being delivered at the time. Non-fitted wagons of this design were converted to fitted under the auspices of BR.

Plate 42

NER 12 TON COVERED GOODS VANS

Plate 43

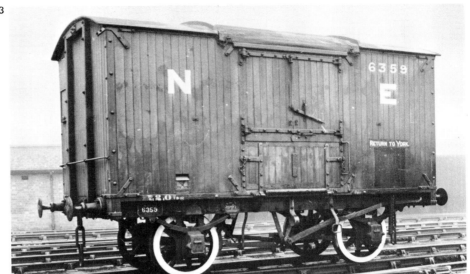

Covered Goods Vans were used for commodities likely to suffer damage if conveyed in open wagons and as such were not nearly as common as open wagons or the mineral wagons to be described next. The North Eastern Railway was the only constituent of the LNER to build vans of 12 ton capacity and these were produced in very considerable numbers. Plate 43 shows one in its NER livery in 1912, while in plate 44 the van has been repainted in LNER style. Both illustrations and figure 18 depict the design with a canvas cover over part of the roof to enable goods to be loaded direct by crane. A number of companies adopted this feature, but by grouping it had fallen out of favour, no doubt due to the difficulties of maintaining watertightness. Note the two varieties of door handle and step irons.

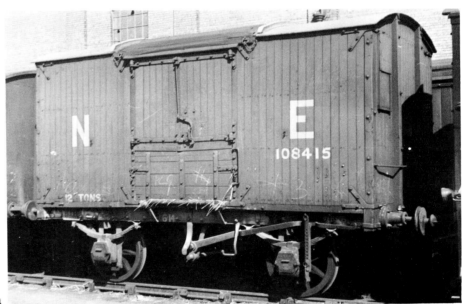

Plate 44

Figure 18

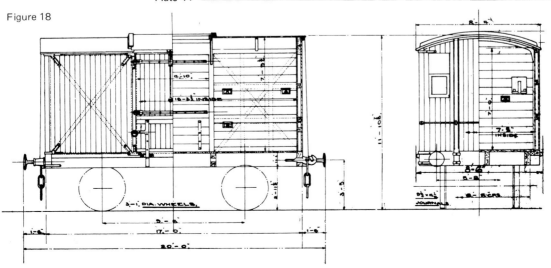

H & B 10 TON VENTILATED VANS

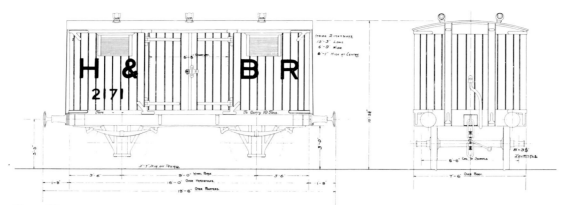

Figure 19

Plate **45**

When compared with other pregrouping companies' designs those of the Hull and Barnsley Railway appear outdated. But the company had only been taken over during the year prior to grouping by its awesome neighbour the NER and H & B vehicles continued in use on the LNER for some time. Figure 19 and plate 45 show non-fitted vans, the latter with sliding doors. Plate 46 is of the vacuum brake fitted version and this example photographed just after the war, is at the end of its life. The running numbers prefixed HB can be seen in both cases.

Plate **46**

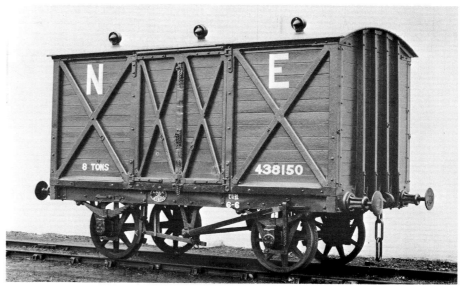

Plate 47

Plate 47 is of a 16 foot long 8 ton van with outside timber framing typical of many companies' older designs, while the four end posts are a sign of its Great Northern origins. Constructed at Doncaster in 1900 this van is fitted with grease axle boxes.

Plate 48 depicts one of the GN's many varieties of 6 ton vacuum fitted ventilated vans built for express goods traffic. It was 16 feet long, had flush sided planking, but still with the four end posts, and two roof vents. Another version with sliding doors is represented in plate 49. This one was 18 feet over headstocks and the wheelbase increased from 9 ft. 6 ins. to 10 ft. Note the two kinds of 'V' hanger used, the assymmetrical one on the right being an LNER replacement.

Plate 48

Plate 49

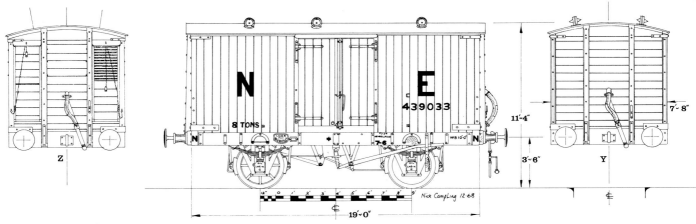

Figure 20

Plate 50

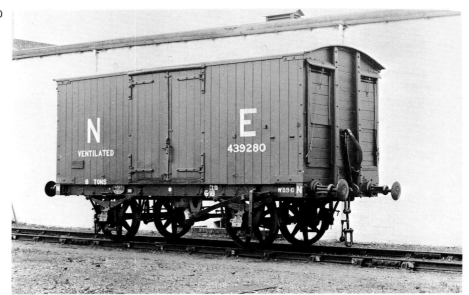

Following the increase in length the capacity was raised to 8 tons, first with a wheelbase of 9 ft. 10 ins. as depicted in plate 50 of a ventilated van built at Doncaster in 1907. As well as six torpedo roof vents, there were two adjustable sliding shutters at each end to give increased ventilation if required. Figure 20 shows the next development with a 2 inch increase in wheel base to the neat figure of 10 feet. These vans were built with plain ends as drawn in view 'Y' or with shutters as view 'Z'. On all the above vans the two outer pairs of roof vents are in line across, but the centre pairs are staggered such that the nearer is always over the left hand door. Similar unfitted vans were supplied to the CLC and rated at 10 tons load.

The final GN design shown in plate 51 did not actually appear until after grouping and these vehicles include many details which arise as a result of the RCH's moves to standardise wagon components. The body is mounted on a 17 ft. 6 in. long steel underframe of 9 ft. wheelbase. Many were built by outside contractors.

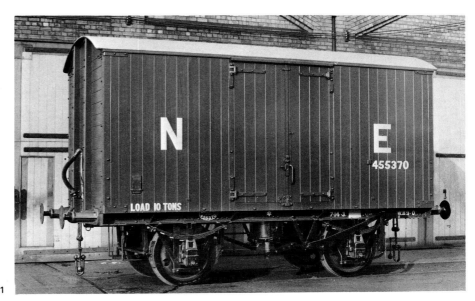

Plate 51

GC AND GE VANS

Plate 52

A few 16 ft. long GC fitted covered vans were converted to 8 ton insulated vans and that in plate 52 is marked 'Return to Parkeston Quay' and therefore no doubt set aside for a specific traffic from the Continent.

Much more common was the 10 ton sliding door vans introduced in 1912, as depicted in plate 53. As with many GN and GC designs examples were built for the CLC. In addition, this one was produced in an automatic vacuum brake fitted version. Deliveries, both unfitted and fitted, were made by Metro-Cammell during the first years of the LNER's existence.

Figure 21 is of a GE 10 ton ventilated van described overleaf.

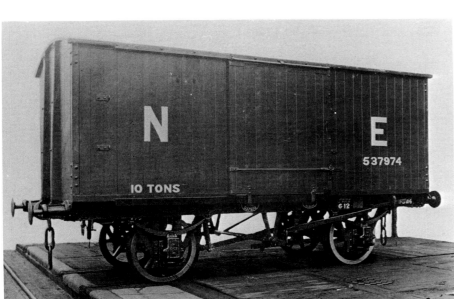

Plate 53

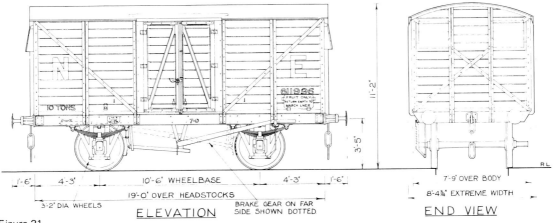

ELEVATION

END VIEW

Figure 21

1'-6'   4'-3'   10'-6' WHEELBASE   4'-3'   1'-6'

19'-0' OVER HEADSTOCKS

3'-2' DIA WHEELS   BRAKE GEAR ON FAR SIDE SHOWN DOTTED

7'-9' OVER BODY

8'-4¾' EXTREME WIDTH

11'-2'

3'-5'

Plate 54

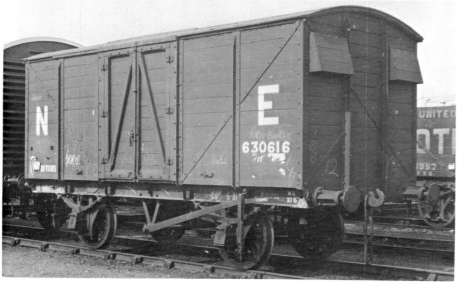

Plate 55

The outside timber framed 10 ton ventilated van built at Stratford in 1900 in plate 54 had become fairly rare by the time this photograph was taken at Stewarts Lane (SEC) about 1937, although many could still be found in departmental service on Great Eastern territory.

Considerably more numerous were the vans depicted in plates 55 and 56, of which there were actually two varieties with lengths over headstocks of 19 ft. 3 in. and 19 feet. Examples of this type have lasted up to recent years in obscure corners of the Engineers' yards. Plate 56 is of a vacuum brake fitted vehicle and shows the later style of lettering. Some of these vans were fitted with roof vents and used to convey fresh meat, while the LNER converted others to banana vans.

Plate 56

NB 10 TON SLIDING DOOR VANS

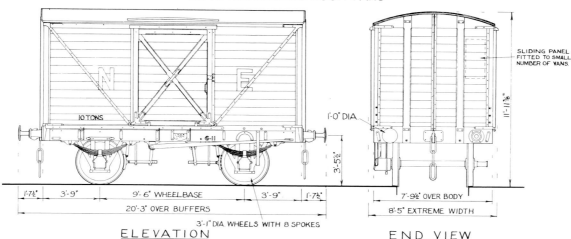

Figure 22   ELEVATION   END VIEW

Plate 57

After the NER 12 ton covered goods van, this North British 10 ton sliding door van was one of the few pregrouping designs found in substantial numbers. Figure 22 and plate 57 show the non-fitted version, while that in plate 58 is equipped with automatic vacuum brakes. The van in plate 57 was built at Cowlairs in 1915 and photographed at Cardington in October 1937. There are several features peculiar to the NB, such as the arrangement of the sliding door, the two timber and one tee iron end posts and the brake gear to the fitted van. The three support brackets to lower door runners are not shown on the original drawings and it is assumed these were deemed to be necessary and added during the life of the vehicle. Examples of the non-fitted version were also to be found mounted on steel underframes.

Plate 58

Plate 59

NB AND GNS COVERED GOODS VANS

An early design of NB van is seen in plate 59 of an 8 ton covered van marked 'RETURN TO SINGER'. This van has the two timber end posts similar to the previously mentioned sliding door van, but no tee iron. It was also fitted with internal bracing. Note the replacement boards on the left hand side following recent repairs, nonetheless the van appears already to have been withdrawn from service.

The NB also used a number of 15 ton six wheeled vans as shown in plate 60 of such a vehicle at Cambridge in July 1952. A number of design features are common with the 10 ton van, although the independent each side brake fitted between the centre and right hand wheels is an unusual variation.

Plate 61 shows a Great North of Scotland 10 ton van with outside framed body mounted on a steel underframe. Note the peculiar spring trunnions, grease axle boxes and that the headstock is of channel section face outwards thus requiring hardwood timber packing pieces between it and the buffer housings.

Plate 61

Plate 60

Plate 62

The LNER's first design of covered goods van with a 9 ft. wheelbase was produced in both automatic vacuum brake fitted and unfitted versions and each came on both timber and steel underframes. Plates 62 and 63 are of the unfitted version and illustrate some of the variations in detail. For instance, notice how spoked and disc wheels could be fitted and the use of broad plate or thinner cranked upper and lower corner strapping pieces. In addition, No. 167449 built in 1932 has a vertical plate bolted over the cranked corner piece and square ends to the headstocks, while No. 151217 has a lamp bracket which is unusual on a non-fitted vehicle.

Plate 63

LNER 12 TON FITTED VANS

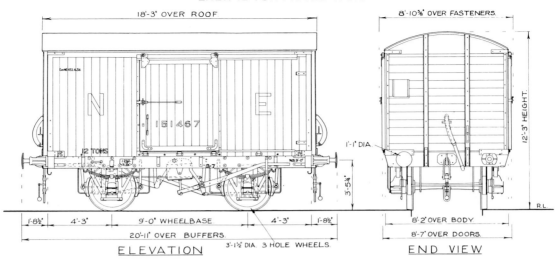

Figure 23

ELEVATION

END VIEW

Plate 64

Figure 23 shows the AVB design of van on timber underframe and 9 ft. wheelbase, while plate 64 is a similar van on a steel underframe and built in 1930. This one has the exterior sliding shutters on the ends reminiscent of the NER vans that preceded them. This feature should be compared with the small opening in the ends of the other vans fitted with the interior shutter.

Late in 1934 the need to increase the wheelbase realised itself in the van depicted in plate 65, but otherwise they were similar to the previous examples. However, more than 1,200 were converted at York to fruit vans by the addition of louvred ends in place of the lower planks and removal of the shutter, the fitting of roof ventilators and 'FRUIT' cast iron plates on the door. See page 39.

Plate 65

LNER 12 TON FITTED VANS WITH STEEL ENDS

Plate 66

With the change to steel underframes for AVB fitted vans initiated in 1934, the decision was made to follow the LMS and use pressed corrugated steel ends as well. This then was the start of the considerable run of vans with this familiar detail. There were, however, as we shall see, several variations and we commence with plate 66 of the type without end ventilators. This photograph of No. 175939 taken at Cardington in November 1938 has been included to remind readers that only the occasional van from each batch posed in front of the official photographer, the remainder went straight into revenue earning traffic and after a few years all became dirty, faded and covered with various chalked inscriptions.

Plate 67 shows the van end modified to include a hooded ventilator. Both these vans were 8 ft. 2 in. over the body and to afford greater route availability and entry to restricted sidings, the body width was reduced by two inches on subsequent construction, as shown in figure 24. At the end of the year 1940 there were 2,998 of these vehicles and the figure increased to 7,700 by the end of the LNER's separate existence, by which time they also had 2,344 with hand brake only. Some of the fitted vans were partitioned inside and used for particular traffics, while others were used for a time at least as fish vans.

Plate 67

Figure 24

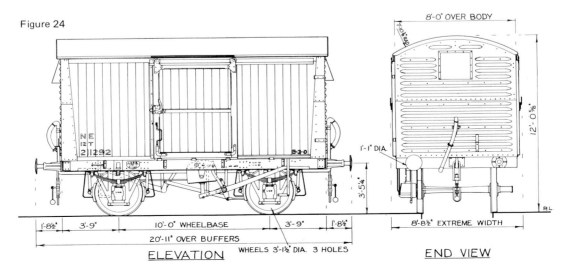

ELEVATION

END VIEW

Plate 68

Plate 68 is an example of a van built in 1937 to the design shown in figure 24. Some later vans had the pressed steel ends in three pieces, instead of two and the letters 'XP' and 'WB 10-0' stencilled above the tare weight at the lower right hand corner of the body, indicating that they could be worked in passenger trains at average speeds exceeding 40 m.p.h.

The shortage of steel during the last war forced a change in design and while keeping the steel underframe a reversion to the all wooden end was made, as illustrated in plate 69 of No. 236824 at Renfrew in September 1946.

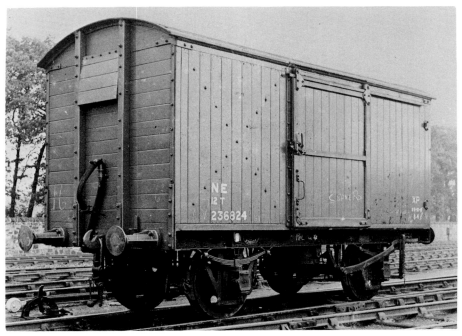

Plate 69

Plate 70

LNER 12 TON VANS

The final design of LNER covered goods van reflected the shortage of materials during and after World War II, and plates 70 and 71 illustrate two unfitted vehicles basically built to the same design, but respectively clad in plywood and narrow vertical match boarding. The first is of No. 265436 in ply at Redhill (SEC) in June 1951, while the second is an official view of the match boarded version built in 1944.

The plywood van also appeared with automatic vacuum brake and plate 72 shows what must have been one of the last vehicles added to LNER stock prior to nationalisation the date being 19th December 1947. Note the pressed steel axle box covers fitted to all these vans, while the first has a builder's plate fashioned from the same material.

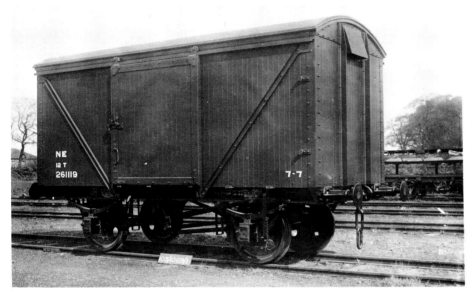

Plate 71

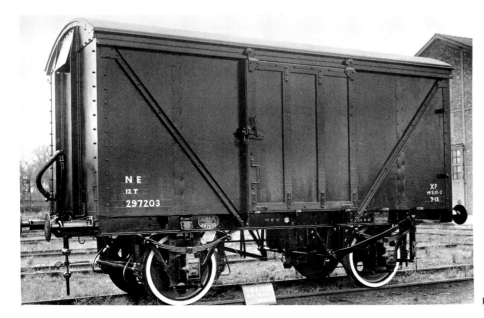

Plate 72

37

FITTED FRUIT VANS

Plate 73

We now come to various classes of van provided for specific traffics requiring some special features and rapid conveyance to avoid deterioration or contamination. The first of these are fruit vans and plate 73 is of a GN 5 ton example fitted with vacuum brake and Westinghouse brake. It was built at Doncaster in 1893 and as well as the two louvred panels in the lower sides, louvres stretched the whole length beneath the roof eaves. In addition, there were roof ventilators and a louvred clerestory.

If you are wondering why the cattle truck in plate 74 is included amongst fruit vans, take a close look at the notice board at the right hand end, which reads 'FRUIT ONLY, Return empty to HULL, LNE'. It seems that, being short of stock to convey fruit traffic, the LNER pressed this newly constructed cattle truck into service, therefore avoiding the risk to hygiene that might have been the case with vehicles from traffic. Such notice boards were common on fruit vans and the three clips, if not the boards, were to be found on many fruit vans. The boards could no doubt be changed as the exigencies of traffic demanded and the following centres are known to have been referred to:- Peterborough, Hull, March and Whitemoor. Alternatively, during the slack periods, the boards could be removed and the van used in ordinary traffic.

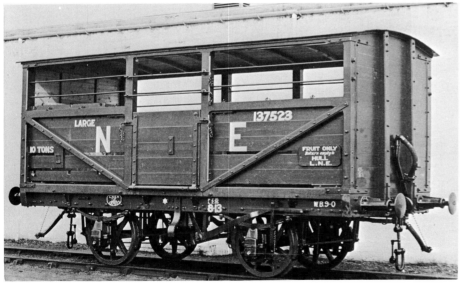

Plate 74

Plate 75 illustrates the position of the torpedo roof ventilators on fruit vans and the like. Note how the centre pair are not on the centre line, but each is slightly offset in opposing directions.

Plate 75

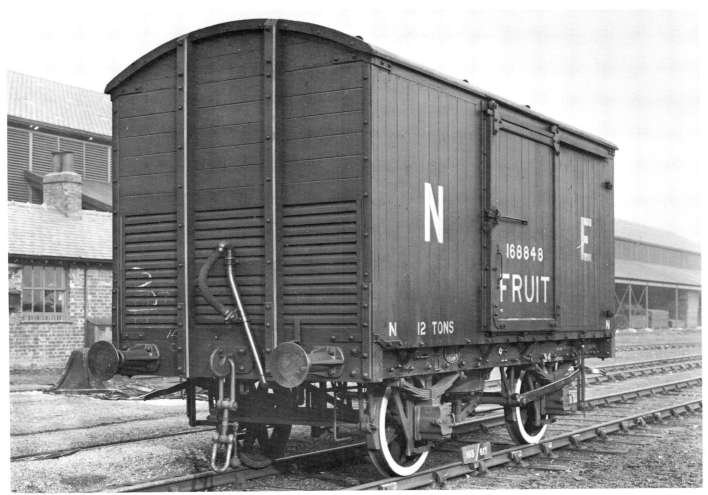

Plate 76

Plate 76 clearly shows louvres in the lower part of the end of a 9 foot wheelbase van. The cast iron plates reading 'FRUIT' have not yet been introduced and the word is painted in 12 inch letters on the door. Plate 77 is of a similar van, No. 174395 built at Darlington in 1934, shows it in traffic in November 1939. Being brake fitted all fruit vans were painted in red oxide.

Plate 77

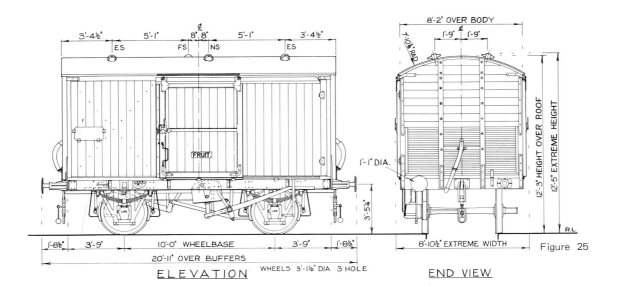

ELEVATION   WHEELS 3'-1½" DIA. 3 HOLE   END VIEW   Figure 25

12 TON FRUIT VANS

Developments in design of the covered goods van were often marked by similar changes in specialist vans, including the fruit vans. The move to steel underframes was easy enough, but clearly pressed steel ends were not applicable and the conventional timber louvres in the ends continued. Figure 25 shows the 8 ft. 2 in. wide version, while plates 78 and 79 are of vans reduced in width to 8 foot over the body.

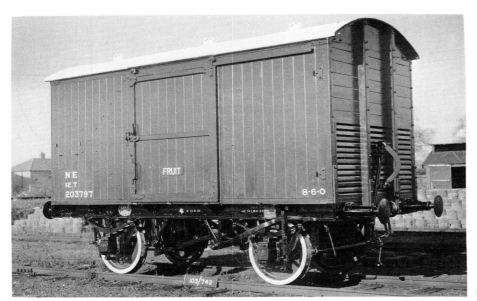

Plate 78

Plate 79

40

LNER 12 TON PLYWOOD FRUIT VANS

Plate 80

The plywood van had its equivalent among the last fruit vans produced by the LNER and during early British Railways days, as plate 80 and figure 26 demonstrate. The photograph is of such a vehicle registered at Darlington and probably built at one of the works in the area in 1945.

Figure 26

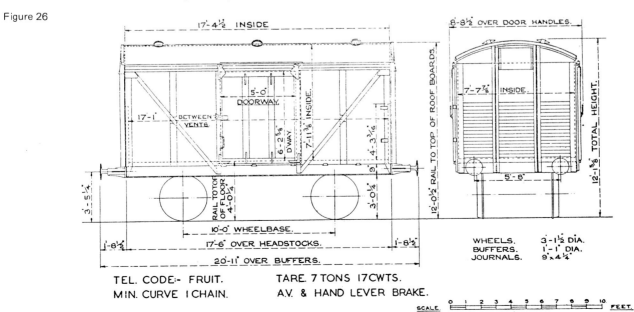

TEL. CODE:- FRUIT.
MIN. CURVE 1 CHAIN.

TARE. 7 TONS 17 CWTS.
A.V. & HAND LEVER BRAKE.

10 TON PERISHABLE GOODS VANS

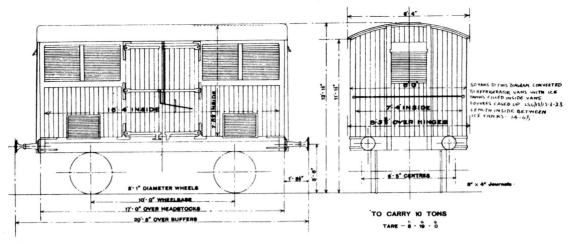

Figure 27

Plate 81

Similar vans on the North Eastern Railway were known as perishable goods vans and as well as fruit could be used to convey fresh meat. Figure 27 is a reproduction of the NER diagram for a 10 ton design introduced in 1909, while the note on the right hand side tells us "50 vans to this diagram converted to refrigerator vans with ice tanks fitted inside vans. Louvres cased up LS6/13/13 - 3 - 23. Length inside between ice tanks = 14' 6½"."

A development of the design with sliding doors but still clearly of NER origin in the underframe is depicted in plate 81 of a van built in 1924. The LNER made further batches with 9 foot wheelbase on both timber and steel underframes and plate 82 shows one of the latter constructed in 1931. Note that both have through steam pipes and vacuum brakes for use in passenger trains, an indication of the importance attached to transporting this type of traffic with the utmost haste.

Plate 82

NER AND GN FISH VANS

Plate 83

It is perhaps difficult to appreciate that fish traffic was conveyed on the railways at one time in open fish trucks, although the boxes or tanks were usually sheeted over, and covered fish vans only began to be used from the turn of the century. Plate 83 depicts a NER 10 ton fish van in its original livery in 1911. It is equipped with both the Westinghouse and vacuum automatic brake.

In plate 85 there is an open fish truck built by the GN in 1897 to carry a removable fish tank. As can be seen these open trucks lasted until after grouping, but when there was an urgent need for brake fitted container flats this dual-braked type was quickly converted, see page 70.

The GN's covered fish van is to be seen in plate 84. Note its double sliding doors, slattered upper half to the sides and that again it is provided with both types of automatic brake and through steam pipe. Although clearly only another development of the covered van and therefore numbered with freight stock and included in the wagon diagram book, in traffic fish vans were treated more as non-passenger coaching stock and their telegraphic codes will be found in the NPC lists.

Plate 84

Plate 85

Plate 86

Plate 87

Plate 86 shows the well known GC 15 ton bogie fish van, after the louvred sides had been replaced by slats. Equipped with AVB, worked by twin cylinders and piped through for Westinghouse brake and steam heating, these vans were mounted on pressed steel underframes and bogies. Note the odd axle box cover to the inner axle of the right hand bogie.

The long van in plate 87 started life as a 15 ton vacuum fitted covered goods van, but this type was downrated to 12 ton capacity and transferred for use as fish vans in 1923. Most had steel underframes, but a few were in timber. Some were also provided with steam pipes.

The more usual 18 foot long 10 ton fish van is represented by figure 28 and is drawn with vacuum and Westinghouse brakes, although not all vans had the latter.

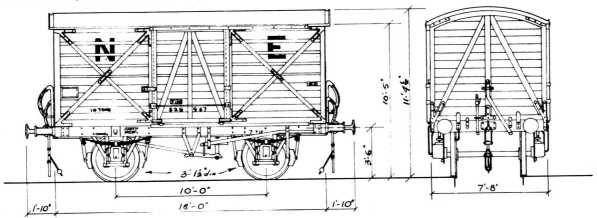

Figure 28

Plate 88

Plate 89

LNER 10 TON VENTILATED FISH VANS

Early batches of LNER fish vans were built with outside framing to the body-work and fully ventilated. In the first example in plate 88, this was simply by means of gaps left between the upper planks. The length of the van is, however, interesting, being 23 feet over headstocks with a 14 foot wheelbase, a trend that was not pursued further until a decade later. The double doors should be noted, together with AVB and through steam pipe. Fish traffic was often worked by passenger train or special fully fitted fish trains.

In plates 89 and 90 the more usual fish van, with louvres in the upper portion of the sides, can be seen mounted on the conventional 9 foot wheelbase 17 ft. 6 in. long timber underframe. All these vehicles were built at Doncaster in 1927 but, whereas the first two were photographed when new, the third was taken at Renfrew in August 1946, after its demotion from fish to an ordinary covered goods van.

All fish vans were provided with slates framed and mounted on the sides where the destination could be chalked, though plates 90 and 92 show that they were not always used.

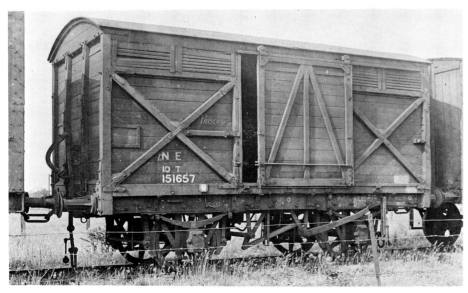

Plate 90

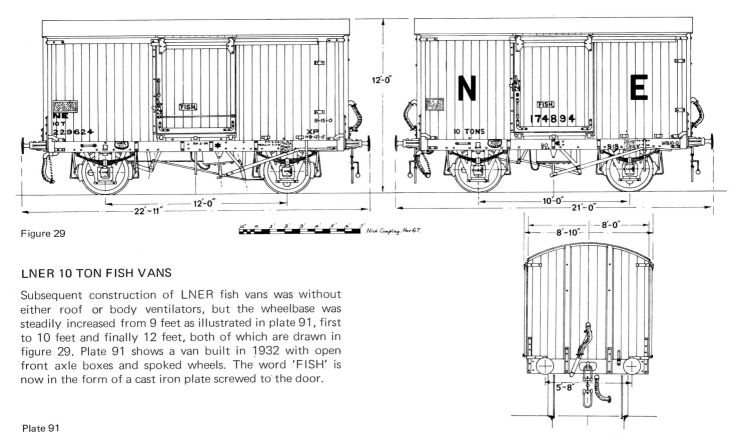

Figure 29

12'-0"

22'~11" 12'-0"

NE
10 T
229624
FISH
9-15-0
XP
WB·12'·0

N   E
10 TONS
174894
FISH
10'-0" 21'-0"
9-15 WB·10'·0

8'-0"
8'-10"
5'~8"

Nick Campling. Nov 67.

LNER 10 TON FISH VANS

Subsequent construction of LNER fish vans was without either roof or body ventilators, but the wheelbase was steadily increased from 9 feet as illustrated in plate 91, first to 10 feet and finally 12 feet, both of which are drawn in figure 29. Plate 91 shows a van built in 1932 with open front axle boxes and spoked wheels. The word 'FISH' is now in the form of a cast iron plate screwed to the door.

Plate 91

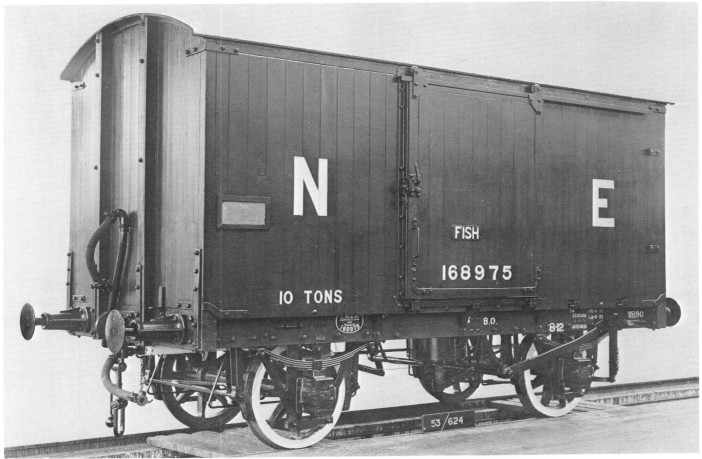

N   E
FISH
168975
10 TONS
B.O. 8·12 WB90
53/624

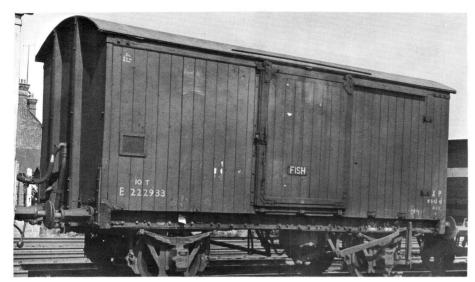

Plate 92

Plate 93

A 19 ft. 6 in. long 12 foot wheelbase fish van is seen in plate 92 in British Railways livery at Bournemouth Central in August 1962. Apart from the 'E' prefixing the number in place of the 'NE' on a line of its own above the load, it is very much as built, although it is thought that the rain strips over the doors were later additions. Numbers for this type included 229145 to 230883 built around 1938. The long wheelbase plywood sided insulated fish vans, familiar with their blue spots, although clearly of LNER design were not in fact built until after nationalisation and therefore outside the scope of this book. However, as plate 93 demonstrates, some of the 12 foot wheelbase vans were also converted to insulated vans with internal sliding doors and painted white. This one was seen by the photographer at Cambridge in August 1952.

Early refrigerator vans were cooled by packing ice in special tanks at each end of the vehicle and for this purpose there were ladders at each end to gain access to the hatches in the roof through which the ice was placed. Naturally rapid transit was called for and the GN van built at Doncaster in 1894 and shown in plate 94 was provided with both vacuum and Westinghouse brakes.

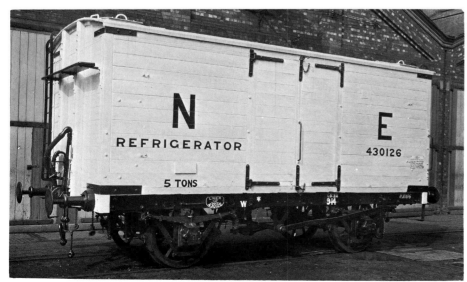

Plate 94

VENTILATED REFRIGERATOR VANS

Plate 95

A later GN refrigerator van built in 1914 is shown in plate 95. Still of 5 ton capacity. It is provided with louvred ventilators in the ends. Refrigerator vans were very distinctive in their white livery, with the solebar and varying amounts of ironwork picked out in black and lettering in black and white depending on the background colour.

The LNER built 8 ton refrigerator vans up to about 1930 in two designs both of 9 foot wheelbase, one with timber and the other steel underframes. The latter is depicted in plate 96 and figure 30. The advent of dry ice, frozen carbon dioxide, and containers saw an end to the need for further refrigerator vans. No. 151275 is interesting in that it was registered at Stratford in 1926.

Plate 96

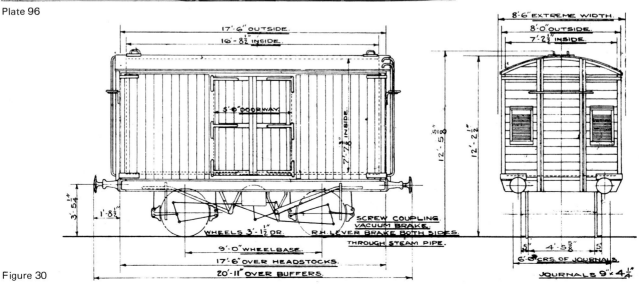

Figure 30

Plate 97

The working of banana trains was a very specialised business, the vans usually running in complete trains from the docks where the bananas were landed to their chosen destination. These vehicles were probably the only goods wagon equipped with steam heating and this was done to ripen the green bananas on their way to market. Plates 97 and 98 are of such vans both built in 1929 with timber underframes and 9 foot wheelbase. The first is of course new, while the second is at Eastleigh in August 1962. A later design on steel chassis and 10 foot axle centres is drawn in figure 31. Other banana vans were converted from GE 10 ton 19 foot covered goods vans described on page 30.

Plate 98

Figure 31

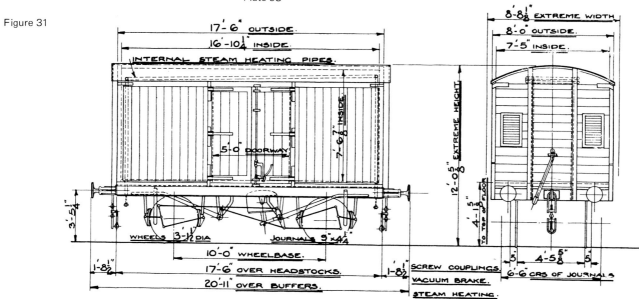

8 AND 10 TON MINERAL WAGONS

Plate 99

Plate 100

A substantial proportion of the LNER's revenue derived from the transport of coal and other minerals and the prime consideration when many of the original lines were promoted was the tapping of this traffic. Depending on their proximity to the coalfields and outlets, together with long established local practices, the pregrouping companies adopted various means of handling coal traffic. In particular extensive use was made of hopper wagons and coal staithes in the north east of England, while elsewhere coal was to a large extent conveyed in wagons owned by the collieries or coal distributors.

The various pregrouping companies had differing ideas on the classification of mineral wagons, some making no distinction between them and open wagons. In this book, if the top board runs through from end to end of the wagon, it is considered to be suitable only for mineral traffic. Many such wagons were provided with top hung end doors to enable them to be un-loaded by end tipping. Plate 99 shows GN and NB examples of this type at Doncaster: the one nearest the camera being a GN 10 ton 5 plank with oil lubricating to the axle boxes.

15'-0½" OUTSIDE
14'-4⅞" INSIDE
8'-0" EXTREME WIDTH
7'-7" OUTSIDE
7'-1¼" INSIDE
7'-2½"
3'-5½"
4'-2" TO TOP OF FLOOR
1'-7½"
WHEELS 3'-1" R·H·LEVER BRAKE BOTH SIDES
5'-8"
8'-6" WHEELBASE
15'-0 OVER HEADSTOCKS
18'-3" OVER BUFFERS
5' 4'-5⅝" 5'
6'-6" ℅ OF JOURNALS
JOURNALS 8" × 3¾"

Figure 32

8 AND 10 TON MINERAL WAGONS

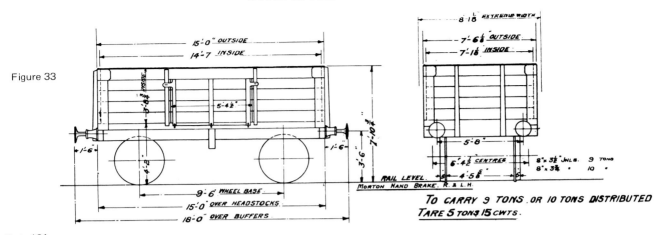

Figure 33

Plate 101

Plates 100 and 101 illustrate another example of the NB 8 ton 4 plank wagon loaded on an LMS implement wagon at Bletchley in June 1939. First introduced by the NB in 1888 they were known as 'Jubilee' wagons and construction continued for a decade or two until they numbered many thousand. Figure 32 is the diagram for this type of wagon.

Figure 33 is a diagram for a GN 9 or 10 ton 5 plank coal wagon, while figure 34 shows a GC 10 ton example with an end door. All these wagons had grease axle boxes and were for the most part withdrawn by nationalisation.

Figure 34

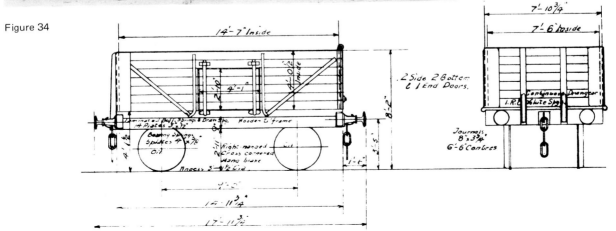

Plate 102

LNER 12 TON END DOOR

Plate 102 shows a 12 ton 6 plank end door mineral wagon built by Clayton Wagon Ltd., of Lincoln to an order placed by the GC. Note the latch to the end door, which is rotated a small amount in a clockwise direction to release the door.

Plates 103 and 104 are of the standard RCH design of 7 plank wagon, used by both the LNER and LMS, together with many private owners. On a timber underframe with split axle boxes, spoked wheels and independent brake gear each side, thus dispensing with the need for a cross shaft which would otherwise foul the bottom doors. The wagon in plate 104 was built by S.J. Claye Ltd., of Long Eaton in 1929. The diagonal stripe across the body side slopes up to the end with the end door.

Plate 103

Plate 104

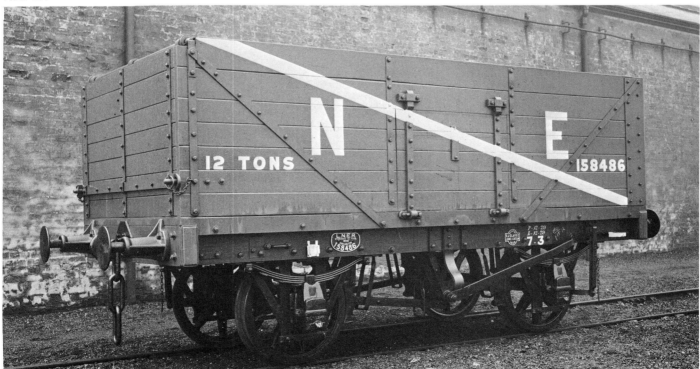

LNER 12/13 TON END DOOR

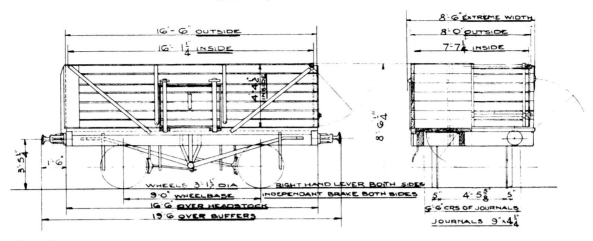

Figure 35

Plate 105

Figure 35 is diagram 10 for the standard 12 ton 7 plank end door mineral wagon and plate 105 is a similar, but later version, seen at Cardington in October 1938. Note the disc wheels, open fronted cast steel axle boxes, later style of lettering and rope hooks on the underside of the kerb rail. Three narrow planks over the door were sometimes used instead of the two broad ones, thus making the wagon into an 8 plank. During the war the LNER found itself with a surplus of end door mineral wagons and many were converted to open wagons, twin bolsters and flat case wagons, see pages 22, 91 and 101.

Subsequently an 8 plank design on a steel underframe was introduced, but still with the 9 foot wheelbase, and this type is illustrated in plate 106 taken at Renfrew in January 1946. Pressed steel axle boxes are fitted, the body work is unpainted except for patches on the bottom plank for the number and tare weight.

Plate 106

53

GN 15 TON AND NB 16 TON END DOORS

Plate 107

The economies in operation to be gained from employing larger capacity wagons had been appreciated by the railway companies for some time, although they did not catch on with many collieries and private owners. Plate 107 is a GN example at Kings Lynn of a 15 ton 8 plank built at Doncaster in 1906.

The NB had substantial numbers of the 16 ton 8 plank wagons depicted in plate 108. Plate 109 shows the typically Scottish end door with the vertical planking, heavy transverse timbers and pair of iron hoops acting as the hinges, while plate 110 illustrates other details of this type of wagon, including the unusual trunnions to the springs and the lower hinge and latch to the cupboard side doors.

Plate 108

Plate 109

Plate 110

NB 18 TON 8 PLANK END DOOR

Plate 111

Having built the 16 ton end door mineral wagon since the first decade of this century, the NB went on in the last few years of its existence to produce an 18 ton version. Massively built, for the most part by contractors, some of these wagons were uprated during the war to carry 20 tons. Plate 111 is of a new wagon built by R.Y. Pickering in 1921. Note the Spencer Moulton buffers, the wharping hook over the left hand wheel, the tie flat between the 'W' irons, the quatrefoil on the door and the inverted crescent inscribed with the year of building to the left hand end. This wagon is in grey livery with the iron-work picked out in black and white tyres to the wheels.

Plate 112 shows another wagon of this design also built in 1921, much later in its life at New England in September 1953. The side doors have been repaired at some time with a single thickness of vertical boarding, instead of the two layers of the original such that on the outside the planks of the door matched the rest of the sides. Figure 36 is a drawing of this type of wagon. This design was also used for NB loco coal wagons.

Plate 112

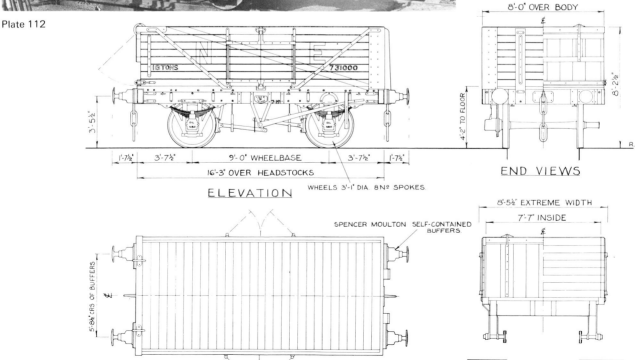

Figure 36

ELEVATION

WHEELS 3'-1" DIA. 8No. SPOKES.

PLAN

SPENCER MOULTON SELF-CONTAINED BUFFERS.

8'-0" OVER BODY

END VIEWS

TYPICAL CROSS SECTIONS

LNER 16 TON STEEL MINERAL WAGONS

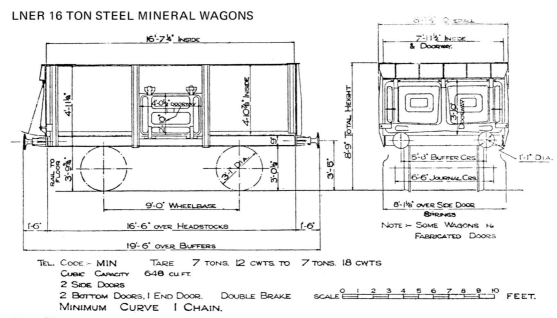

TEL. CODE :- MIN   TARE   7 TONS. 12 CWTS. TO   7 TONS. 18 CWTS
CUBIC CAPACITY   648 CU. FT.
2 SIDE DOORS
2 BOTTOM DOORS, I END DOOR.   DOUBLE BRAKE   SCALE ⊢⊢⊢⊢⊢⊢⊢⊢⊢⊢⊣ FEET.
MINIMUM CURVE I CHAIN.

Figure 37

Following the example set by the Ministry of Transport during the war, both the LNER and LMS put in hand from 1945 the construction of considerable numbers of 16 ton all steel end door mineral wagons with the typical pressed steel side and end doors. Figure 37 and plate 113 illustrate this design, the riveted form of body construction being usual on the LNER. No. 274579 was built by the Teesside Bridge and Engineering Works Ltd., of Middlesbrough in 1945 and by the end of 1947 there were 7,200 wagons to this diagram, numbered in the ranges 270005 to 270703, 271305 to 273103, 274579 to 274977, 279209 to 280208, 287689 to 289188 and 289926 to 291688.

Plate 113

10½ AND 12 TON COAL HOPPERS

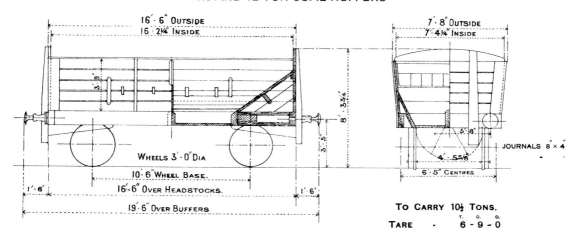

Figure 38

Having dealt with the end door mineral wagons we move on to the hopper wagons used almost to the exclusion of anything else in the north-east of England and to a lesser extent in Scotland. Figure 38 is of a NER 10½ ton 5 plank hopper wagon, of a type introduced late in the last century and built in substantial numbers. The end stanchions were extended downward to allow chaldron wagons to buff up. The latter, although long banished from main lines were often to be found at collieries for internal use. Side brakes or end hand brakes could be fitted.

The NER had developed over the years a complete range of coal hopper wagons of varying sizes and throughout its existence the LNER continued to construct modernised versions. Plate 114 shows a 12 ton 8 plank hopper with straight sides built by the Birmingham Railway Carriage & Wagon Co. Ltd., of Smethwick in 1937.

Plate 114

12/13 TON COAL HOPPERS

Plate 115

Along with most open and mineral wagons the 12 ton design was rated to carry 13 tons from early days of the last war and plate 115 shows such a hopper built in 1941 with the bottom two planks sloped inwards. Notice that much of the woodwork is unpainted and that patches have only been provided for such lettering as was necessary. This wagon was photographed at Eastfield in January 1947.

The next move was to make the whole side sloping and this can be seen in plate 116 of a 13 ton 8 plank built in 1945. The number plate and axle box covers are of pressed steel and self contained buffers have been fitted.

Of similar height but longer was the 17 ton 8 plank coal hopper of NER design, although the one in plate 117 was built by the LNER in 1926. The long brake handles were on both sides but the remainder of the brake gear is on the side nearest the camera only.

Plate 116

Plate 117

58

20 TON COAL HOPPERS

Plate 118

The NER began building 20 ton coal hopper wagons in earnest in 1903, until by grouping there were over 17,000 of them. Initially double 'W' irons were used, but from about 1917 the more conventional single type inside the leaf springs were employed as shown in plate 118 of No. 54143 at Colwick around 1936, by which time it appears to be a cripple or out of regular use. Plate 119 is an end view of the same vehicle and shows the draw hook to be missing. Notice also the massive timber end posts, which in earlier days would have extended down another foot to form drop buffers for use against chaldron wagons. The LNER decided in 1925 to saw these off.

Figure 39 is LNER Diagram 12 of their version of the 20 ton hopper with steel 'T' section end posts, but otherwise very similar to its NER predecessor.

Plate 119

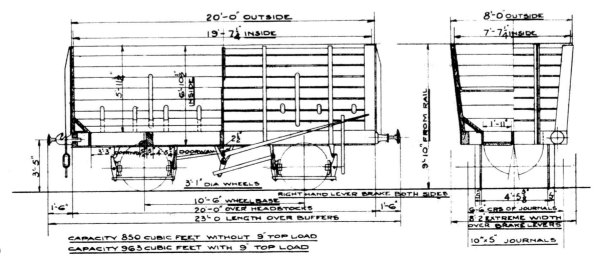

Figure 39

Plate 120

Plate 121

The LNER went on to construct more than 7,000 wagons to figure 39, as illustrated by plates 120 and 121. The latter of ex. LNER wagon No. 182383 seen in May 1968 is in the service of the United Steel Co., at their Workington Steel Works.

Some 20 ton hoppers were converted to carry dust coal to power stations and plate 122 depicts such a vehicle. A light framework has been fixed over the top and covered by a wagon sheet, and dust tight seals fitted on the hopper doors.

Plate 122

Plate 123

LNER 20 TON STEEL COAL HOPPERS

As already mentioned, extensive use was made of hopper wagons for the conveyance of coal in the north eastern area. In 1936 diagram 100, reproduced as figure 40, was prepared and a number of firms invited to draw up their detailed designs for 20 ton hopper wagons of all steel construction. There are therefore differences in detail and plate 123 is Messrs. Hurst Nelson & Co. Ltd.'s version built in 1936, while plate 124 is a view looking down into the hopper of a wagon built by Metropolitan Cammell & Co. Notice the handrail all round the inside.

Plate 124

Plate 125

Plate 125 shows a similar wagon built in 1936 by Messrs. Head, Wrightson & Co. Ltd., of Thornaby on Tees. However, there are differences in the side stanchions, solebar and end handrails. Two bottom doors were provided on all wagons of this type and the operating handles can be seen attached to the solebar each side of the 'V' hanger.

The above companies, together with the Birmingham Railway Carriage and Wagon Co., built 3,355 of these vehicles in three years. Later, others were to join them until there was a total of 8,163 by nationalisation, many of which are still in use today.

Figure 40

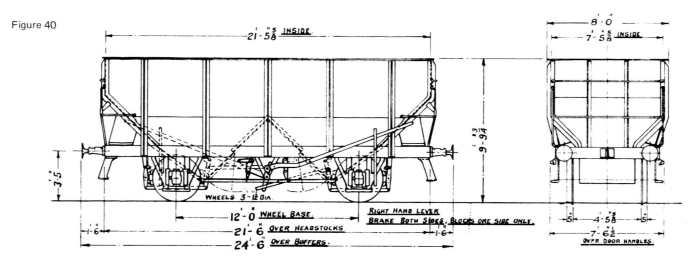

LNER AND MOT HOPPERS

Plate 126

Following the fall of France in 1940 a large number of 20 ton wagon underframes to continental specifications were surplus to requirements and 2,500 were completed as hopper wagons. The hopper plates were 5/16 inch thick, which permitted their use for conveying iron ore and many were used by the MOT for this purpose as plate 126 illustrates. Another seen later in life at Leeman Road, York in June 1972 is reproduced in plate 127. As built there was considerable variation in detail in both types of steel coal hopper wagons and during repairs the various components could be further mixed up until the permutations become innumerable.

Plate 128 shows one of a hundred side discharge hopper wagons built in 1939 for carrying fine washed coal. The canvas flaps over the axleguards are to prevent the coal finding its way into the axle boxes. The series of door latches can be seen mounted along the solebars and actuated by the levers at each end.

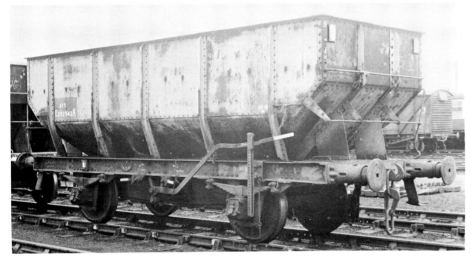

Plate 127

Plate 128

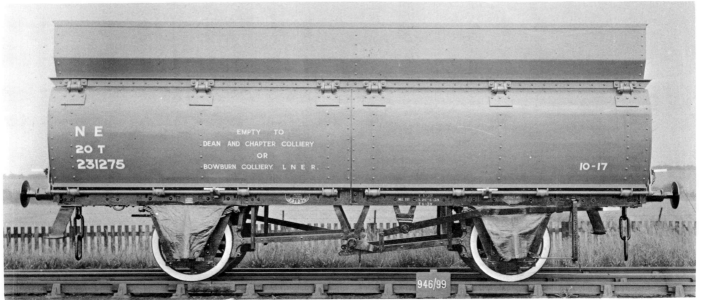

LNER BULK ALUMINA AND SODA ASH HOPPERS

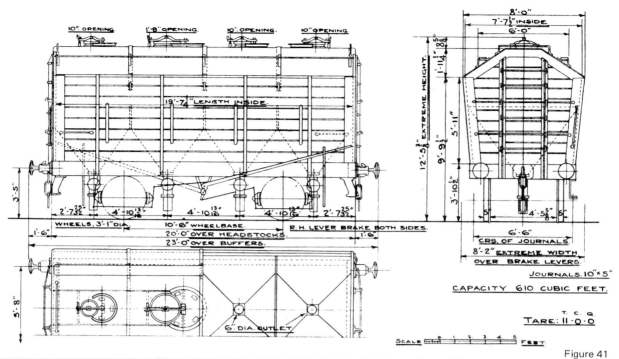

Plate 129

Figure 41

Plate 130

Special wagons were provided for the traffic of alumina from Burntisland on the Firth of Forth. Initially these were converted from 20 ton 8 plank coal hoppers by roofing over and fitting four 6 inch diameter discharge pipes. Figure 41 of Diagram 82 has a pronounced peak to the roof to take advantage of the angle of repose of the powder. When further wagons were required an all steel design was brought out as depicted in plate 129 of No. 229080 built in 1938. Others were numbered between 229067 and 229090.

Similar hopper wagons were used for soda ash, as can be seen in plate 130 of a 20 ton all steel soda ash hopper wagon built at Dukinfield in 1937. This shows extensive use of welding in its construction.

IRONSTONE HOPPERS

Plate 131

Iron ore is another bulk mineral that can well be handled by hopper wagons and in 1905 the NER introduced the 30 ton high capacity design, shown in plate 131. This wagon was actually built a year later and was equipped with each side independent hand brake actuated by levers across each end and is also provided with automatic vacuum brakes. The large discs above each axle box were part of the anti-friction gear used on this and other types of high capacity wagons.

A possibly more rational design introduced in 1909 was the shorter 20 ton wagon illustrated in plate 132. Note the double hornplates to the axle boxes.

The LNER produced two very similar designs of 25 ton ironstone hopper wagons, the only difference being in the brake mechanism. Figure 42 shows the one with side lever brake, 80 of which, Nos. 204697 to 204776, were built in 1937 by Messrs. Craven Railway Carriage and Wagon Co.

Plate 132

Figure 42

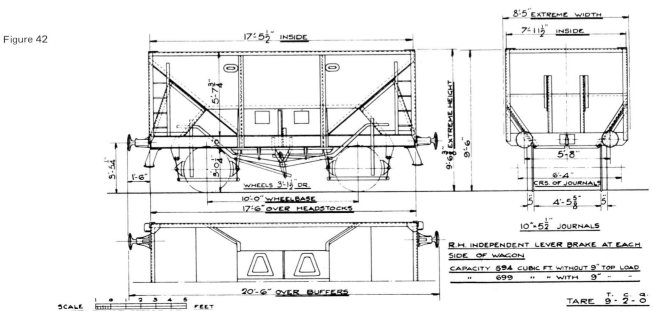

Plate 133

LNER 25 TON IRONSTONE AND 20 TON GRAIN HOPPERS

Subsequent construction of 25 ton ironstone hoppers had the end mounted hand brake depicted in plate 133. Numbers included 269946 to 269990, 274326 to 274352 built in 1946 and 300020 to 300213, the last few of which were probably delivered to BR.

The original batch of twenty five 20 ton convertible bulk grain wagons delivered between September and December 1929 and shown in plate 135 were built to Great Western Railway drawings. The grain always seems to have been taken on at King George Dock, Hull, hence the notice 'Return to Silo, Hull' and destinations included Sowerby Bridge, Chesterfield, Sunderland and Sheffield.

Plate 134

Plate 135

20/22½ TON BULK GRAIN HOPPERS

As plates 134 and 136 demonstrate, the original intention was to use these wagons as either covered goods vans or bulk grain hoppers and the floor was ingeniously arranged with flaps to form either a flat floor covering the discharge chutes, or the hoppers. There were a few problems with this, but as the new design of wagon generated an increasing demand, further batches were built solely as hoppers. Note in plate 134 the inspection windows in the ends, also the lifting eyes in the floor and the rope for transferring the flaps from one position to another.

In its final form the two pairs of side doors on each side were unnecessary and a small inspection door was provided on one side only. Two loading hatches were incorporated in the roof, with steps and handrail at each end. The doors, roof hatches and hand wheel to operate the hopper doors on both types were provided with padlocks, all of which were to be locked before moving the wagon. Plate 137 is of a non-convertible type built in 1931, while plate 138 shows a similar vehicle constructed in 1937, hence the revised livery, and rated to carry 22½ tons. Numbers of the revised design included 164865 to 164884, 187972 to 188006 and 203804 to 203852. A few wagons to this design are still in use at the time of writing.

Plate 136

Plate 137

Plate 138

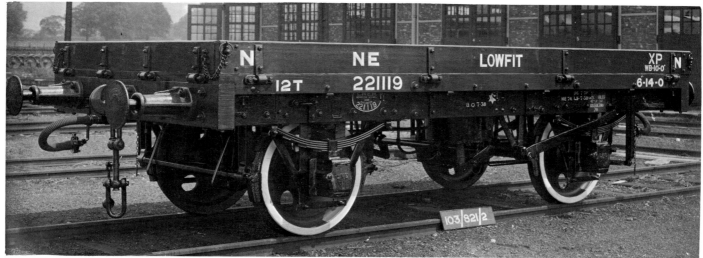

Plate 139

In the mid thirties the LNER built nearly 1,400 single plank fitted wagons with all four sides hinged at the bottom. These wagons could be used for a wide range of individual items such as road vehicles. An example is the RAF's gas bottle trolleys seen in plate 140 at Cardington in April 1940 loaded on 'Lowfit' No. 203160 built in 1937. Plate 139 shows a similar wagon constructed a year later in its untarnished red oxide livery, while figure 43 is a reproduction of Diagram 109 for this design. It was not intended that these wagons should be used for container traffic and later a notice was painted on to this effect.

Plate 140

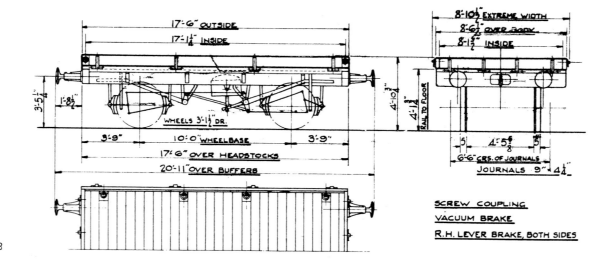

SCREW COUPLING

VACUUM BRAKE

R.H. LEVER BRAKE, BOTH SIDES

Figure 43

LNER 12 TON CONTAINER FLATS

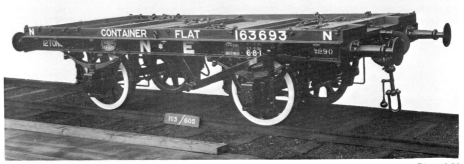

8'-6" EXTREME WIDTH
7'-3½" BETWEEN CHOCK PLATES
5'-8"
4'-5⅝"
5"   5"
6'-6" CRS. OF JOURNALS
JOURNALS 9" x 4¼"

4'-6"
3'-10" RAIL TO FLOOR

3'-5¼"
1'-8½"
WHEELS 3'-1½" DIA.
10'-0" WHEELBASE
17'-6" OVER HEADSTOCKS
20'-11" OVER BUFFERS

SCREW COUPLING
VACUUM BRAKE
R.H. LEVER BRAKE BOTH SIDES

FITTED WITH BINDING CHAINS
AND SHOCK ABSORBERS

Figure 44

The railways container business grew from small beginnings soon after grouping until in later years it accounted for a substantial part of their revenue, the LNER building up such traffic on its express goods trains from Kings Cross and elsewhere. The containers themselves were to Railway Clearing House design and initially any suitable open wagon was used to carry them. When purpose built flat wagons were developed by the individual companies, there was a tendency at first to use one variety of container on one type of flat. Later, when further sizes of container were developed, a range of chock positions was incorporated thus affording greater flexibility in traffic. Plate 141 is of an early design of container flat with 9 foot wheel base built in 1932 and wagons to this design were later converted to have the same fixings as figure 44 and plate 143 of a 'Conflat S' to Diagram 104. A dramatic downturn in livestock traffic meant that AVB fitted underframes from surplus cattle trucks could be reused as additional container flats and plate 142 is of such a vehicle built in 1927 and converted into a 'Conflat V' in 1936.

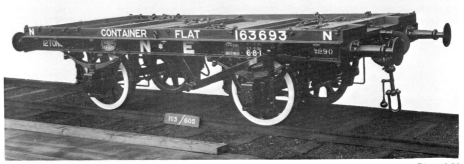

Plate 141

Plate 143

Plate 142

Plate 144

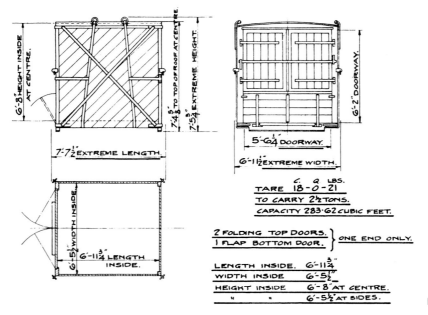

6'-8" HEIGHT INSIDE AT CENTRE.

7'-7½" EXTREME LENGTH.

7'-4⅝" TO TOP OF ROOF AT CENTRE.

7'-5¾" EXTREME HEIGHT.

6'-5⅜" WIDTH INSIDE.

6'-11¼" LENGTH INSIDE.

6'-2" DOORWAY.

5'-6¼" DOORWAY.

6'-11½" EXTREME WIDTH.

C. Q. LBS.
TARE 18-0-21
TO CARRY 2½ TONS.
CAPACITY 283·62 CUBIC FEET.

2 FOLDING TOP DOORS. } ONE END ONLY.
1 FLAP BOTTOM DOOR. }

LENGTH INSIDE. 6'-11¾"
WIDTH INSIDE 6'-5½"
HEIGHT INSIDE 6'-8" AT CENTRE.
"   "   6'-5½" AT SIDES.

Figure 45

The type A container was the smaller of the two basic sizes and in plate 144 No. A105 is seen loaded on a 5 ton container flat converted from a GN open fish truck built in 1909. Note that it is fitted with both vacuum and Westinghouse brakes. Figure 45 is the diagram for the 2½ ton Type A container, from which it may be observed that the doors were at only one end. These early versions of the type A and B containers were painted red oxide, while the roofs and lifting eyes were white.

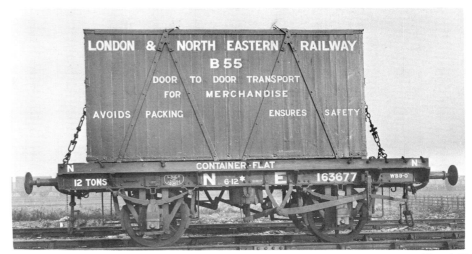

Plate 145

CONTAINERS TYPES B, BC and BD

The other early design of container was the 4 ton type B and plate 145 illustrates one loaded on a container flat and properly chained up for travel by train. The 'N' and 'E' have been reduced in size and painted on the solebar of the flat wagon.

Variations on the basic size were given a suffix letter and plate 146 shows a plywood bodied type BC container specially adapted to carry 78 bicycles and a typical example of the container traffic. Other ordinary merchandise carried was joinery, confectionery, castings, cookers, baths, machinery, stoves, boots, cloth, carpet, tinware, silkyarn, pianos, gramophones, sugar, shrubs, wireless equipment and so on. But, notice that compared with their bulk all items are relatively valuable and some require special care in packing: therefore higher freightage charges were justified by a rapid door to door service.

The BD containers had side doors as well as those at one end and were especially useful when one of the loading or off-loading operations had to be carried out while the container was still on the wagon. Plate 147 is of this type on a 'Conflat S'. Notice that the securing chains have not been attached and that space has been provided at the upper right hand end of the side for traders' adhesive labels — a bit of free advertising. From about 1934 all containers used the Gill Sans lettering and the bodywork is thought to have been Oxford blue.

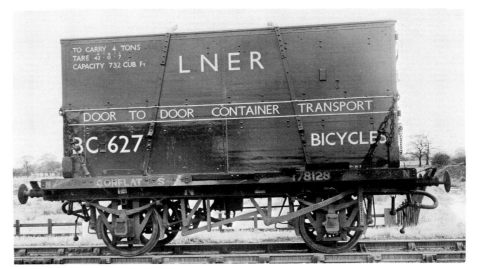

Plate 146

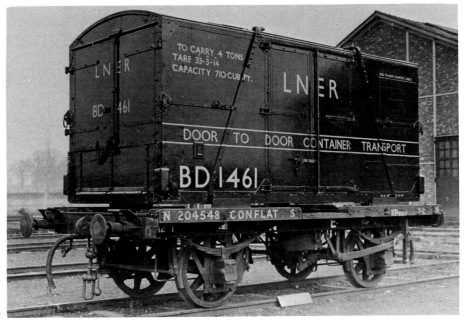

Plate 147

Plate 148

Plate 149

Type BK containers were for household furniture removals. Plate 148 shows the exterior of a newly built container in 1935 on a 'Conflat V' and plate 149 the inside with the end doors open. The doors were split into three with the lower part a drop flap and the upper as two side hung doors. The sides of the interior were fitted with slats for securing the items of furniture in the usual fashion.

Plate 150

CONTAINERS TYPE BK

Plate 150 illustrates a later version of the BK container on its own. By 1938 when this photograph was taken the end door fixing had been changed from the large swinging beam in plates 148 and 149 to the long vertical rotating bolt with a curved arm to engage in the lower door.

Plate 151 is of a similar container loaded on the ubiquitous 'Conflat S' in 1940. The style of lettering depicted was used by all four companies, the background being blue in the case of the LNER, while others followed their express passenger liveries closely with crimson lake with black edging for the LMS, chocolate brown with yellow markings and grey roof for the GW, see *Great Western Wagons Appendix* by J.H. Russell, plate 161 and sea green and yellow script on Southern containers. It must have been too much for the LNER to do theirs out in varnished teak!

Figure 46 is the diagram for a Container BK.

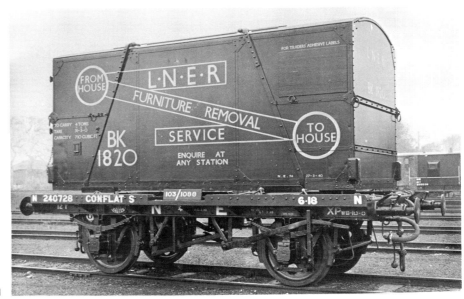

Plate 151

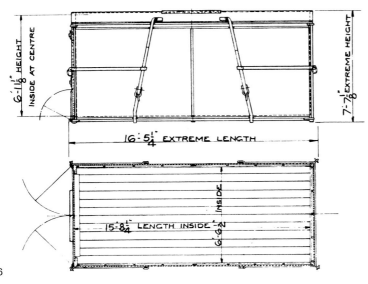

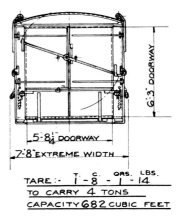

TARE:- T. C. QRS. LBS.
1 - 8 - 1 - 14
TO CARRY 4 TONS
CAPACITY 682 CUBIC FEET

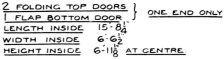

2 FOLDING TOP DOORS
1 FLAP BOTTOM DOOR } ONE END ONLY
LENGTH INSIDE 15-8¼
WIDTH INSIDE 6-6½
HEIGHT INSIDE 6-11⅛ AT CENTRE

Figure 46

CONTAINERS TYPES BP, BLP AND R

In 1929 experiments were made with pressed steel containers and these offered advantages in reduced tare weight, thus enabling them to be loaded fully when on 5 ton wagons. Initially there were problems with condensation and heat build up inside, improved ventilation being called for, Plate 152 is of the 4 ton type BL photographed in Cardington in May 1939. A similar version with removable shelves for perishable goods was known as the type BLS and built with the intention of attracting traffic in the confectionery, the small package business and to assist in securing to rail transport soft fruit going at the time to the jam factories by road.

A slightly later design of steel container with ventilators in the upper part of the sides is depicted in plate 153 of a BLP loaded and secured on 'Conflat S' No. 178053. Notice the shock absorbers at the lower ends of the chains, and lettering indicating that this type of container could be used for Continental traffic by train ferry. In the same way that insulated vans were provided for the conveyance of meat, insulated containers were developed for traffic in imported meat, as shown in plate 154 of a container type R with both side and end doors. As can be seen, this was painted white with black lettering. Matching container flats were built complete with through pipes for steam heating, suggesting that these vehicles regularly worked in passenger trains. The type R container was later rechristened the type F without meat hooks, or FM with meat hooks.

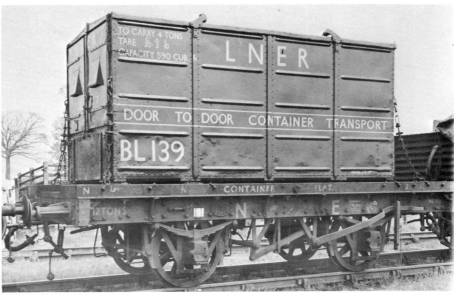

Plate 152

Plate 153

Plate 154

Plate 155

Plate 156

OPEN CONTAINERS

Open as well as covered containers were developed during the interwar period and plate 155 shows a 4 ton type D 5 plank open in grey livery in 1932. Falling doors were provided on both sides and at one end. Spreaders and sheet supports were fitted to keep the sides apart while the container was slung from a crane. Plate 156 is of a later version with 6 planks and in the blue livery, showing all the doors open.

In plate 157 is the type DX, which had 6 plank full length dropsides and ends, the spreaders being removable.

Finally, for small loads, a 2¼ ton type H was produced as a scaled down version of the DX and provided with a lid. In plate 158 two have been loaded in a 3 plank dropside wagon.

Plate 157

Plate 158

Plate 159

Plate 159 shows one of the NB's more numerous designs of 10/12 ton cask wagons for ale traffic. No. 703544, built about 1905 and withdrawn prior to 1938, is seen newly painted in its LNER livery late in 1923. There were still 48 of this type in December 1940 and one lasted into BR days until 1954.

Plate 160 is of a 12 ton longfit wagon built in 1936 and hence wearing the earlier style of lettering with the 'N' and 'E' in large size.

Plate 160

LNER 12 TON LONGFIT PIPE WAGONS

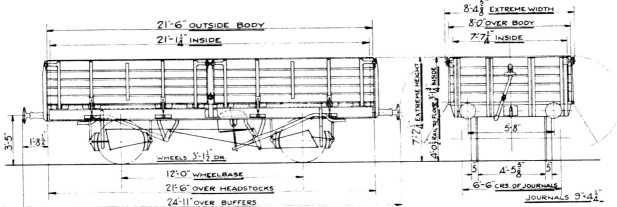

Figure 47

The 12 ton 'Longfit' wagon was designed to carry pipes and most had 'Empty to Staveley Works NE' or 'Empty to Stanton Iron Works, Ilkeston LNE' inscribed on them. They came in two widths, figure 47 of Diagram 103 being of the narrow version 8 feet over the bodywork, while the other was 8 ft. 4 ins. wide at this point. Numbers included 187823 to 187871, 204297 to 204396 and 296945 to 297014, the last few of which were delivered to BR. The first group was probably the narrow design and the remainder wider.

Plate 162 illustrates a very late comer to the LNER, having been out-shopped in December 1947. Note the long link between the widely spaced vee hangers for the AVB gear on a 12 foot wheelbase vehicle.

Plate 161 is the end detail of a NB 10 ton tube wagon described on the next page.

Plate 161

Plate 162

77

TUBE WAGONS

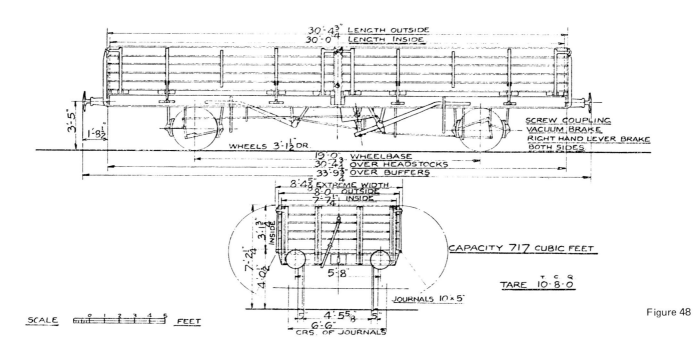

30'-4¾" LENGTH OUTSIDE
30'-0¼" LENGTH INSIDE

3'-5"
1'-8½"
WHEELS 3'-1½" DR.

19'-0" WHEELBASE
30'-4¼" OVER HEADSTOCKS
33'-9¾" OVER BUFFERS

SCREW COUPLING
VACUUM BRAKE
RIGHT HAND LEVER BRAKE
BOTH SIDES

8'-4¾" EXTREME WIDTH
8'-0" OUTSIDE
7'-7¼" INSIDE

7'-2¼" INSIDE
3'-1½" INSIDE
4'-0½"

CAPACITY 717 CUBIC FEET

T C Q
TARE 10-8-0

5'-8"

JOURNALS 10 × 5"

4'-5⅝"   5"
6'-6"
CRS. OF JOURNALS

SCALE |0 1 2 3 4 5| FEET

Figure 48

For traffic in steel tubes the NB developed a long fixed sided wagon as depicted in plate 163 of a 10 ton wagon at Kings Cross in the late '30s. A detail of the end is also to be found in plate 161 on the previous page.

The LNER produced 20 ton designs with fully fixed sides and also two part dropsides. Figure 48 of Diagram 98 and plate 164 illustrates the latter version equipped with automatic vacuum brake gear. Note the inclined stays to the lower ends of the 'W' irons, and round push rods to the brake shoes instead of the more usual flat section.

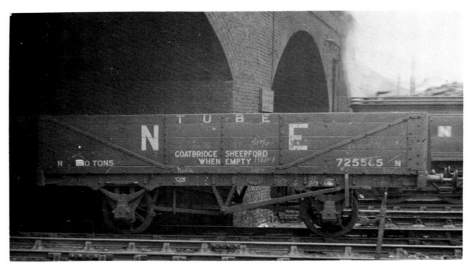

N TUBE E
COATBRIDGE SHEEPFORD
WHEN EMPTY
N 20 TONS
725565 N

Plate 163

Plate 164

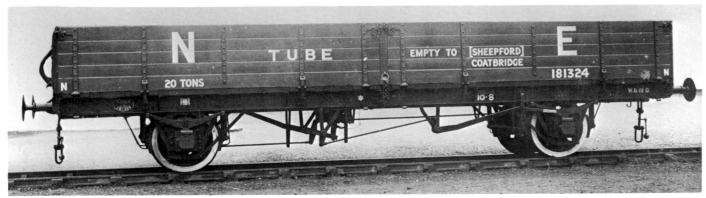

N TUBE EMPTY TO [SHEEPFORD] E
COATBRIDGE
20 TONS 181324
N 10-8 W.B.19-0 N

GN 9 TON AND LNER 12 TON PLATE WAGONS

Plate 165

Probably the commonest wagon for carrying the products of the nation's steelworks was the plate wagon. Plate 165 is a GN version of 9 ton capacity built at Doncaster in 1914 and equipped with grease lubricated axleboxes. This type was all but extinct by nationalisation.

The LNER's plate wagons were of an all steel design, initially of 12 ton capacity and riveted construction. Plates 166 and 167 are of vehicles of this type built in 1930 and 1936 respectively, the first has split and the other the cast steel open fronted axleboxes. Numbers included 170770 to 171246 and 184091 to 184286.

Plate 166

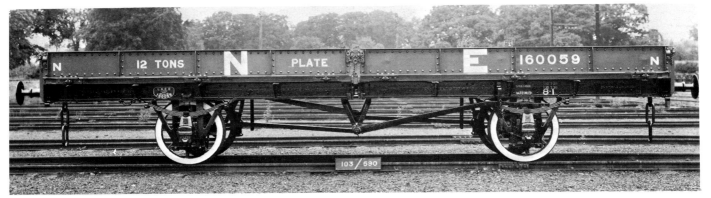

Plate 167

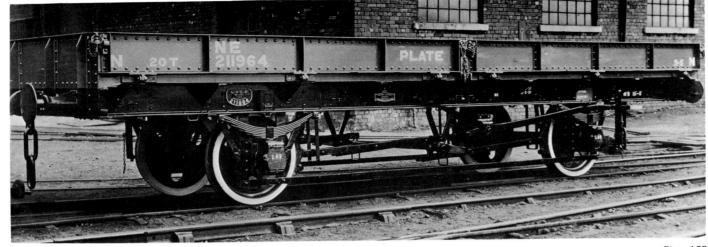

Plate 168

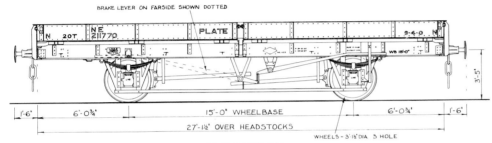

BRAKE LEVER ON FARSIDE SHOWN DOTTED

N   20T   NE   211770   PLATE   9-4-0   N

WB 15'-0"

3'-5"

1'-6"   6'-0¾"   15'-0" WHEELBASE   6'-0¾"   1'-6"

27'-1½" OVER HEADSTOCKS

WHEELS - 3'-1⅛"DIA 3 HOLE

ELEVATION

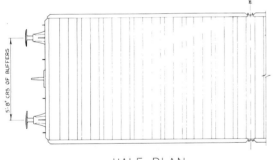

5'-8' CRS OF BUFFERS

HALF PLAN

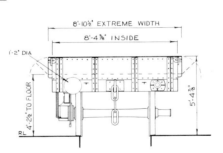

8'-10½" EXTREME WIDTH

8'-4⅜" INSIDE

1'-2" DIA

4'-2½" TO FLOOR

5'-4⅜"

RL

END VIEW

Figure 49

In 1937 the capacity of plate wagons for new construction was increased to 20 tons, as illustrated in figure 49 and plate 168. As can be seen riveted construction continued for a while. No. 211964 was built in 1937 by Messrs. Craven Railway Carriage and Wagon Co., others of the batch were made by the Cambrian and Pickering. Numbers included 211765 to 212757, 239569 to 240068, 242219 to 242462, 250846 to 251397, 265885 to 266099 and 286490 to 286608.

Plate 169

Plate 170

As continuing advances were made in welding techniques these were used in wagon construction and as plate 169 shows the plate wagon made an ideal example, although some riveting remained in the underframe. No. 239569 was built in 1940 and plate 170 illustrates the wagon with the door down. Note the removable centre post between the two doors and the raised wooden slats to keep the steel plates up off the floor and enable lifting hooks to catch the plate edges during loading and off-loading.

After the war the LNER introduced a brake fitted version of the plate wagon, as depicted in plate 171 of such a wagon built in 1947. Numbers for these were 292095 to 292344.

Plate 171

Bogie plate wagons are strictly speaking specially constructed vehicles, but it is felt preferable to discuss them here as a natural progression of the four wheeled plate wagons. As SCVs the code is followed by a letter which identifies the exact design of wagon referred to and in figure 50 and plate 172 we see a 'Boplate B' acquired from the Government as war surplus by both the NER and later the LNER. No. 139512 photographed at Cardington in May 1939 was built by the Gloucester Railway Carriage & Wagon Co., the builder's plate being just to the left of the centre line, while the inscription to its left reads: 'to be returned to nearest L.N.E. principal shops Sept. 1940'.

The numbering of all 32 NER wagons was entirely random, and the LNER's 216 were a little 'hit and miss', however some of the sequences were as follows:– ex. NER 4989, 4991, 91053, 91061, 91064 and the LNER 139489 to 139492, 139562 to 139578, 139602 to 139607, 139610 to 139617, 139456 to 139488, 139493 to 139545 and 147516 to 147530.

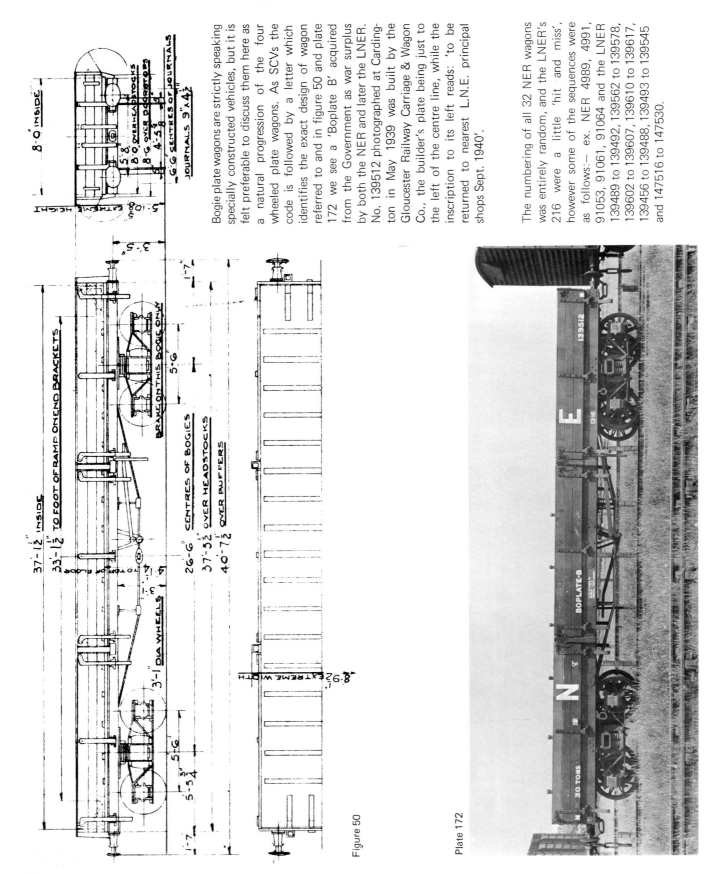

Figure 50

Plate 172

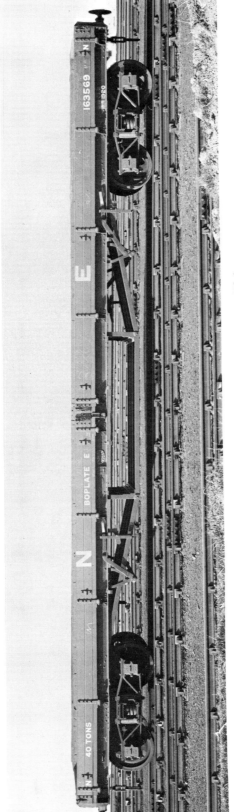

Plate 173

The LNER's only design of bogie plate wagon was 52 foot long over headstocks and of 40 tons capacity. It had steel ends and 2 plank dropsides divided into two parts on each side of the vehicle. Plates 173 and 174 both show No. 163569 built by Metropolitan Cammell Carriage and Wagon Co. Ltd., of Birmingham in 1930. The underframe and bogies are identical to the 40 ton bogie bolster 'Quint Ds' to be described on page 93.

The numbers of the 'Boplate Es' as the wagons were coded, were 163560 to 163659 and 228892 to 229063, the latter being built around 1938.

Plate 174

NER 8/10 TON SINGLE BOLSTERS

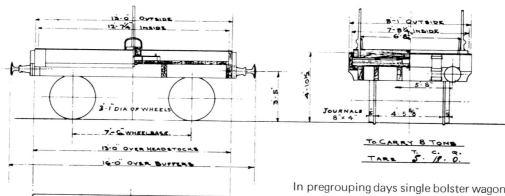

Figure 51

In pregrouping days single bolster wagons were used to carry all manner of long loads from bulk timbers and rails to fabricated steelwork and boilers. At grouping the NER had 2,717 8 ton and 5,725 10 ton single bolsters, of which 3,033 remained at nationalisation.

The loading of single bolsters called for considerable skill and forethought. As plate 176, taken at Doncaster demonstrates a rigid load placed on more than two bolster wagons is liable to come to grief on going round curves. Note the displaced packing on the left hand wagon. The three wagons are all NER 8 ton single bolsters with grease lubrication. The right hand one with dumb buffers and wooden brake blocks was probably withdrawn from revenue earning service prior to grouping.

Figure 51 is Diagram D2 of a NER single bolster wagon equipped with a swivel bolster, which could be lowered when positioned longitudinally, thus enabling the wagon to be used as a runner or match under a long load. Plate 175 shows a 10 ton example in BR days at Huntingdon North in September 1952.

Plate 175

Plate 176

Plate 177

Plate 178

All the constituent companies of the LNER had single bolster wagons, although in less profusion than the NER. Plate 177 is a GN 9 ton example resplendent in its recently applied LNER livery in 1925. Note the chains neatly secured round the bolster pins. Plate 178 depicts No. 503905, the GC's 10 ton version on a steel underframe at Colwick around 1936. Whilst in plate 179 we have a GE 10 ton bolster wagon No. 612239 built in 1908 and seen at Newark. This one is of steel construction with only a wooden floor and bulk timber bolster. Note the private owner wagons in the background.

The proper loading of wagons was the subject of a booklet of instructions and much of this was devoted to the correct use of single bolsters and match wagons for transporting rigid loads. All four railway companies issued similar instructions and interested readers are referred to the *Railway Modeller* Vol. 18, 1967, pp. 170-171 for further details.

Plate 179

NB AND SINGLE BOLSTERS

Plate 180

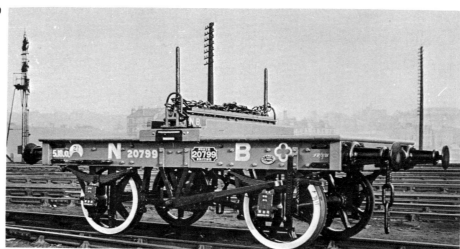

The NB 10 ton single bolster wagon was without sides and had a steel bolster with only a timber rubbing piece on top, as can be seen in plate 180 of No. 20799 in 1921 in its pregrouping livery.

The LNER 12 ton single bolsters were to several diagrams, but all were 15 ft. 6 in. over headstocks and of 8 foot wheelbase. The earlier ones generally followed the NER design, as plates 181 and 182 indicate. No. 204783 was built in 1937 by Messrs. Chas. Roberts & Co. Ltd., and has the unusual interim livery still retaining the large company initials, but the load and number are to the left end and tare weight to the right on the kerb rail. No. 240531 was built three years later and had the conventional later style of lettering, but note the spoked wheels.

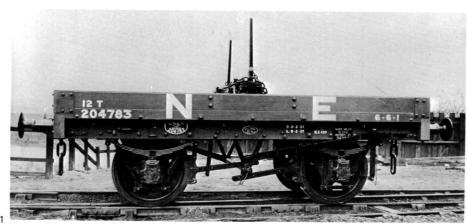

Plate 181

Plate 182

86

LNER 12 TON SINGLE BOLSTERS

Plate 183

Plate 183 is a view looking down on an LNER single bolster and clearly shows the arrangement of the swivelling bolster and 'D' links to which the securing chains are attached.

250 wagons were made as shown in plate 184 with steel underframes and No. 213095 was built at Dukinfield in 1937.

The final LNER design for single bolsters was an all steel one and plate 185 illustrates an example constructed in 1946.

Plate 184

Plate 185

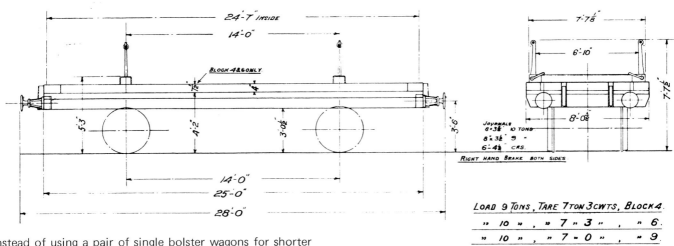

Figure 52

Instead of using a pair of single bolster wagons for shorter loads of a rigid nature, two bolsters mounted on a single four or six wheeled vehicle known as a double bolster wagon could be employed.

Figure 52 and plate 187 are of GN double bolsters. As can be seen from figure 52 there were both 9 and 10 ton versions and the latter came with two heights to the sides, the 9 ton being the more numerous. The rings and light chains from the top of the bolster pins seem to be peculiar to GN bolster wagons. No. 438017 was built at Doncaster in 1900.

The GC 10 ton double bolster, as illustrated in plate 186, is in many ways similar, but is mounted on a steel underframe and has oil lubricated split axle boxes. Note also the squared rather than the rounded 'D' shackles at the ends of the bolsters, and the inscription 'Rail and Timber' painted on the side.

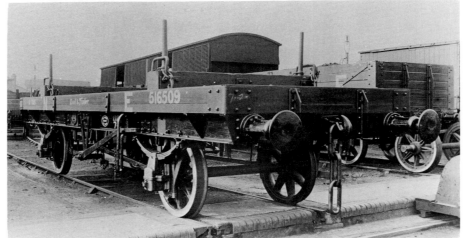

Plate 186

Plate 187

Plate 188   LNER 12 TON DOUBLE BOLSTERS

Plate 189

The LNER's first design of double bolster clearly shows its NER origins with both pins at the ends of the bolsters and secondary pins along the sides. Of 12 ton capacity it was mounted on a steel underframe and incorporated many RCH standard parts. The initial batches had bulk timber bolsters as depicted in plates 188 and 189, later a pair of rolled steel channels placed back to back were substituted as shown in plate 190 and figure 53 (overleaf).

No. 135347 was made at Dukinfield in 1924. Despite its five digit number 88866 was built in 1929 and must be one of the last examples of reusing vacant numbers, while 184559 was constructed in 1936 and has the cast steel open fronted axle boxes.

Plate 190

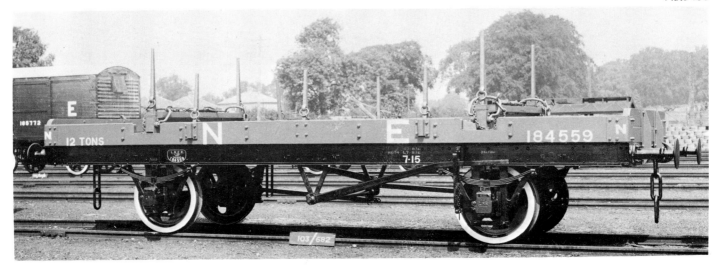

Plate 191

Figure 53

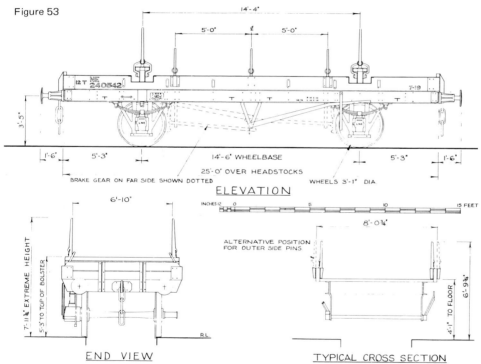

14'-4"

5'-0" ₵ 5'-0"

12 T NE 240542

T T T T

T-19

3'-5"

1'-6" 5'-3"

14'-6" WHEELBASE

25'-0" OVER HEADSTOCKS

BRAKE GEAR ON FAR SIDE SHOWN DOTTED

WHEELS 3'-1" DIA

ELEVATION

5'-3" 1'-6"

6'-10"

INCHES 12 0 5 10 15 FEET

7'-11¾" EXTREME HEIGHT

5'-3" TO TOP OF BOLSTER

ALTERNATIVE POSITION FOR OUTER SIDE PINS

8'-0¾"

6'-9¾"

4'-1" TO FLOOR

RL

END VIEW

TYPICAL CROSS SECTION

12 ton double bolsters with the revised bolster detail continued to be built up to about 1941 and a drawing is re-produced in figure 53. Numbers included 184538 to 184912 and 240374 to 240652.

Subsequent construction of double bolsters was to a 21 ton all steel design very similar to the 20 ton plate wagon with the addition of a pair of bolsters and indeed these were removable and the sides of the falling type. An example, built in 1943, is illustrated in plate 191.

Permanently coupled wagons for carrying long loads were called twins and in plate 192 we see a pair built by Messrs. Hurst Nelson for the NB in 1911. Two pins were attached to each side of both wagons, which could be raised as shown or lowered into the brackets fixed on the side plank. The wagons were equipped with simple brakes and grease axle boxes.

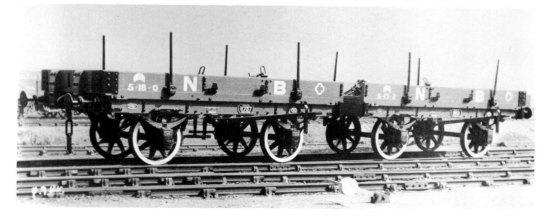

Plate 192

Plate 193

Plate 193 is a composite picture of a GC twin bolster set loaded with telegraph poles at Bletchley in June 1939. Each wagon was capable of carrying 10 tons and plate 194 shows the detail of the permanent coupling between the steel underframed wagons.

A sudden need during the War for further twin bolster wagons was met by converting surplus 12 ton mineral wagons, by then rated at 13 tons, see page 53. Plate 195 shows a 7 and an 8 plank from which the side and end doors have been removed and swivel bolsters fitted, but still loose coupled. Other wagons had the sides removed as well and subsequently some were close coupled and had the bolsters moved towards the centre thus necessitating a reduction in load to 9 tons per wagon.

Plate 194

Plate 195

NER AND NB BOGIE BOLSTERS

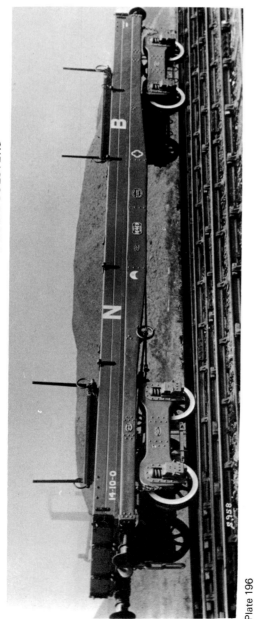

Plate 196

As with the plate wagons the bogie bolsters are actually 'Specially Constructed Wagons' about to be discussed: however, as bogie bolsters are a natural development of the single, double and twin bolster wagons, they will be dealt with here. Plate 196 is of a NB 30 ton 45 foot long swivel bolster coded 'Gondola'. Only two bolsters were provided, but these could be used in any of three positions – as shown and also on the centre line of the wagon. Later these were removed and the wagons used for carrying steel plates. Numbering was somewhat random but included the following runs:- 727403 to 727410 and 727412 to 727422.

Plate 197

The NER was the only other constituent company to own bogie bolster wagons of which it had several varieties. Plate 197 shows a 40 ton 'Quint C' No. 129067 built after grouping at York. It was photographed at Dorchester South in September 1952. The code gives the clue to the number of bolsters, in this case five. There were also 'Quads' and a single example of a 'Treble'. The load of tree trunks, after steelwork, is typical for such wagons. A trussed underframe with diamond bogies is to be seen on this wagon, but other 'Quint Cs' were as illustrated in plate 234 of such a wagon converted into a 'Trestle G'. Numbers were J951 to J986, J989 to J998, M972 to M983 and 129001 to 129120. NER letters J and M became 117xxx and 120xxx respectively as wagons passed through the shops from 1922.

LNER 40 TON BOGIE BOLSTERS 'QUINT D'

From 1929 the LNER introduced its own design of 40 ton 52 foot long bogie bolster, known as 'Quint D', as shown in figure 54 and plates 198 to 201. Plate 198 is of No. 227822 built by Messrs. R.Y. Pickering.

Plate 198

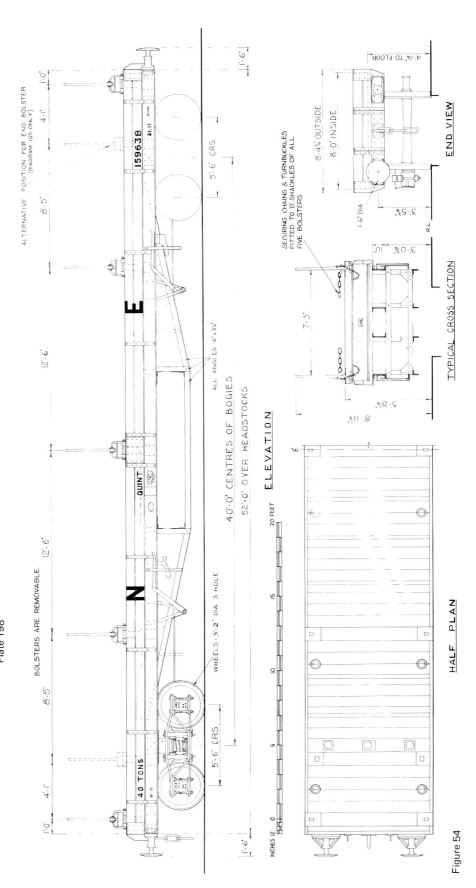

ALTERNATIVE POSITION FOR END BOLSTER
(DIAGRAM 105 ONLY)

159638
21.11

BOLSTERS ARE REMOVABLE

ALL ANGLES 4" × 3½"

WHEELS - 3'-2" DIA 3 HOLE

40'-0" CENTRES OF BOGIES

52'-0" OVER HEADSTOCKS

ELEVATION

INCHES 12   0   5   10   15   20 FEET

SECURING CHAINS & TURNBUCKLES
FITTED TO 'D' SHACKLES OF ALL
FIVE BOLSTERS

4-1¼" TO FLOOR

8'-4¾" OUTSIDE
8'-0" INSIDE

1'-2" DIA

3'-5¾"

END VIEW

TYPICAL CROSS SECTION

HALF PLAN

Figure 54

93

LNER 40 TON BOGIE BOLSTERS 'QUINT D'

Plate 199

The initial batches of 'Quint Ds' had only five positions for the bolsters, although these were removable. Their numbers were 129121 to 129220, 153181 to 153300 and 159437 to 159736 to diagram 38. Subsequent construction to diagram 105 had an alternative position for the outer bolsters over the bogies and began with 188507 to 188606 built by various contractors in 1936, followed by 227822 to 227921 in 1939. Slats on the floor were also provided, so that plates could be carried once the bolsters had been taken off.

Plate 199 is of No. 188507, the first of the modified design, built in 1936 by Messrs. Metropolitan Cammell Carriage and Wagon Co. Ltd. Note that the bolsters are in the inner position and the wagon has been painted in the interim livery current just at that time. Plate 200 shows in close up the details of No. 188593 near the end of its life in Wimbledon Yard in April 1968. The arrangement of the bolster pin, chains and shackles should be observed, together with the distinctive shape of the reinforced buffer housing used on several designs of larger LNER wagon.

Plate 200

Plate 201

Plate 202

Plate 201 depicts 'Quint D' No. 159604 in 1941, having been repainted in the revised livery. The inscription 'Bogie Bolster. — D' on the bottom plank appears to have been recently applied and must be part of a national code for special vehicles of this type and is the code subsequently adopted by BR. On the solebar to the right of the centre is painted "to be returned to the nearest NE area principal shops Dec. 1942". A similar note is to be found on the wagon in plate 198.

The LNER also had a few 60 foot long 40 ton bogie bolster wagons with seven bolsters, coded of course 'Sept'. Certain features of the design, illustrated in plate 202, are common to the 'Quint D' but the wheel diameter was smaller than standard at 2 ft. 9 in. and instead of the two plank sides, a steel bulb angle section was used, a detail not adopted on the 'Quints' until shortly after nationalisation. The first 'Septs' numbered 129221 to 129225 were built in 1928 and were followed later by 203853 to 203867.

Plate 203

Specially constructed vehicles are those wagons which were purpose built for carrying heavy or outsize loads. As such they could not be used without proper supervision and their movements were closely monitored by Central Wagon Control at York who were advised daily of their whereabouts. The LNER had a very broad definition of this type of vehicle and included all bogie wagons, such as the bogie bolster and plate wagons already mentioned, in this category. These vehicles were relatively few in number, but attracted attention because of their form of construction and the unusual loads carried. A separate diagram book was issued for SCV's as early as 1926 and this shows all pre-grouping vehicles with their running numbers and loading restrictions. It was of course kept up to date by the issue of amendments as necessary.

Plate 203 shows a number of these vehicles made up into a special train to transport a pair of very large plate girders on their sides and which are undoubtedly an 'out of gauge' load. This means that the size of the load is such that it would foul the adjacent line on double track sections especially on curves and great care will be needed in passing bridges and other lineside obstructions. Such loads are therefore only moved under 'possession' of the track at slack periods at night or more probably on Sundays when other traffic can be halted or diverted. In this view the load is resting on a pair of armour plate wagons equipped with swivel bolsters and spaced by a selection of implement, low machine and flat wagons.

Plate 204

Plate 205

One of the simplest forms of specially constructed vehicle was the implement wagon, which with a reduced diameter of wheel permitted a lowered floor, upon which farm implements and the like could be placed and secured by ropes to rings in the floor. Plates 204 and 205 are of GN examples. The first is a 10 ton 'Imp N' No. 404861 built in 1914, and one of 129 taken over by the LNER. The six wheeler is the sole example of a 20 ton 'Imp X' 22 ft. 1 in. long produced at Doncaster in 1902. Note the unusual brake levers reaching to ratchets on the underside of the headstock.

When it was required to convey taller loads a lower machine wagon was called for and another GN wagon is illustrated in plate 206. This is of 18 ton capacity 'Mac D' built in 1903. Note the unusual tie rods attached to the side plates. Numbers were 425232 to 425239. Much more numerous was the GE's 14 ton 25 ft. 6 in. long 'Mac K' of which there were 162 at grouping, 83 lasting to nationalisation, after which BR built 52 new to basically the same design.

Plate 207 depicts No. 621620 carrying an ingot shortly after the war. Other numbers were 621603 to 621624, 621651 to 621730, 621903 to 621922, 621933 to 621952, 621954 to 621963 and 621991 to 622000.

Plate 206

Plate 207

NER 20 TON 'MAC L' AND LNER 20 TON 'MAC NV'

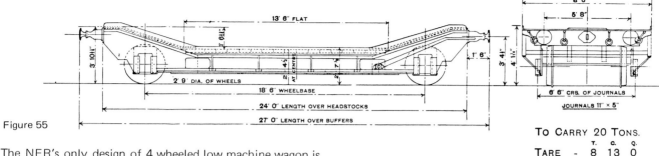

Figure 55

TO CARRY 20 TONS.

TARE - 8 13 0

The NER's only design of 4 wheeled low machine wagon is shown in figure 55 and plate 208. Of 20 ton capacity numbers 68932, 5444, 72948 and 22792 were built in 1913 and were followed later by 9228, 10294, 18084, 27807, 76804 and 78854. No. 68932 is seen in the photograph after the war loaded with an ex. SECR 7 plank open wagon without springs.

Plate 209 illustrates an LNER 'Mac NV' new in 1939 and figure 56 is Diagram 143 for this design, which seems to have been developed from the GC's 'Mac N' with the addition of AVB. They were numbered 230913 to 230967.

Plate 208

Plate 209

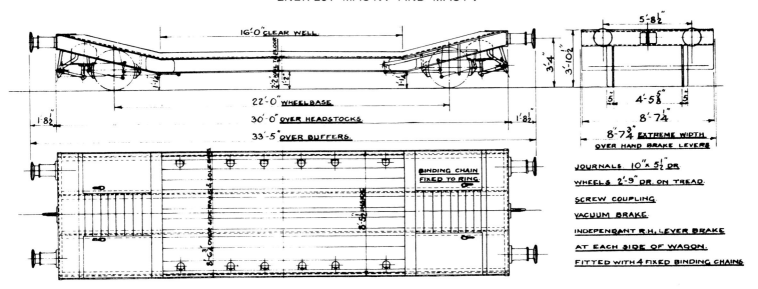

Figure 56

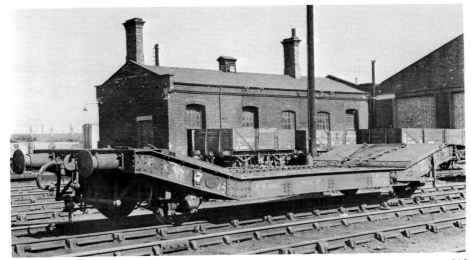

Plate 210

The capacity of the 'Mac NV' was raised to 22 tons with the general increase early in the war, but subsequent construction was for 25 ton loads which necessitated a deeper section for the side members, resulting in the 'Mac PV'. Plate 210 depicts No. 260855 at Peterborough in May 1953. The arrangement of the vacuum brake gear fitted at each end was the same for both designs and details are shown in plates 211 and 212 of 260848 at Poole in March 1973. Numbers were 260848 to 260877, 263274 to 263298 and 278484 to 278508. A further 30 wagons being added in BR days.

Plate 211

Plate 212

Plate 213

Plate 214

Plate 215

Plate 216

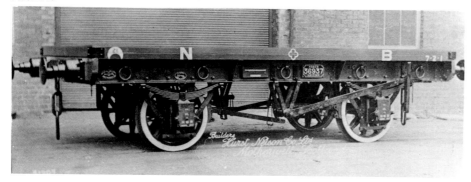

After the First World War 40 surplus WD 35 ton 'Rectank As' were acquired by the NER and put into traffic. Numbers were entirely random, but the LNER built a further batch of 'Rectank Bs', numbered 229091 to 229102. However both plates 213 and 214 are of 'Rectank As', Nos. 12811 and 20600 respectively. These wagons were designed to carry tanks which could be loaded from an end dock. To support the tanks' weight as they drove over, pairs of jacks were provided under the headstocks and queen posts and plate 214 shows the former. The 'Rectank B' was to a revised design with smaller diameter wheels giving a floor 6 inches lower, the tie rods were replaced by angle section and jacks were only fitted to the headstocks. Small but wide loads were conveyed on flat wagons of which there was a considerable variety of types each of a few vehicles. Because the loads might project over the sides and the care needed in securing them, these wagons were subject to the instructions relating to specially constructed vehicles. Plate 215 is of a GN 9 ton 'Flat A' of which there were 50, while plate 216 shows the NB equivalent of a 20 ton 'Flat H', numbered 736935 to 736937.

Plate 217

For the conveyance of wide flat cases further 12 ton mineral wagons were stripped of their bodywork, equipped with a pair of bolsters and coded 'Flatcase'. Plate 217 shows No. 224065 so converted.

Fifteen 27 foot long AVB fitted flat wagons were also built in 1939 and plate 218 is of No. 228083. These were numbered 228077 to 228091. Another 32 were added by BR.

Plate 218

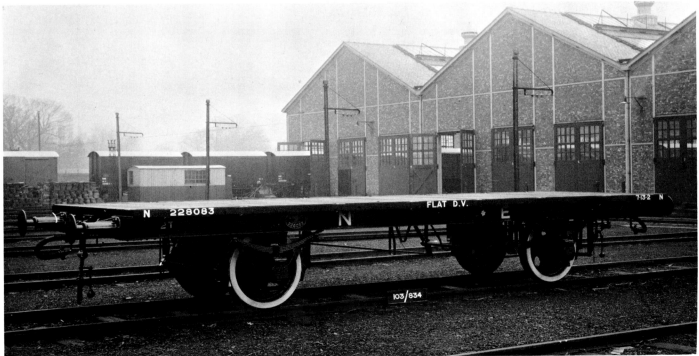

Plate 219

Large flat wagons were bogie vehicles and plates 219 and 220 depict 55 ton 30 foot long 'Flat Ts'. The first is No. 217330 after the war and the other shows a close up of a stator seated on timber baulks and secured by binding chains to No. 217295 built by the LMS at Wolverton in 1938 to Lot 1144. These and some other SCV's appear to have been designed and built as a joint venture with the LMS shortly before the last war. Certainly the bogie is a typical LMS design. LNER numbers were 217295 and 217329 to 217331, while similar LMS vehicles carried the numbers 700201 to 700203.

Plate 220

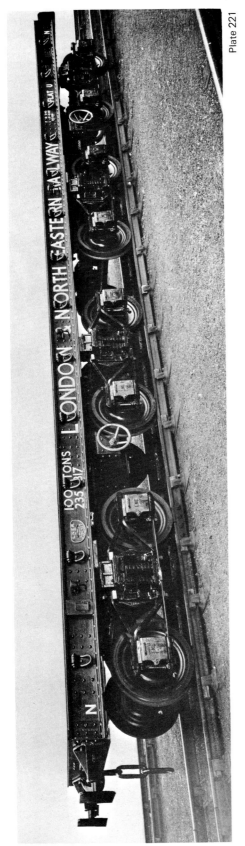

Plate 221

The largest flat wagon was the 44 foot long 100 ton 'Flat U' of which there was only one example, No. 235317 built in 1940 and illustrated in plate 221. Two pairs of bogies are mounted on two individual sub frames which are free to rotate under the main frame, but the load is transmitted through bearers between the top of the bogie and the underside of the solebar. Note how some advertising has been indulged in by writing 'London & North Eastern Railway' in full along the solebar.

Plates 222 and 223 are of bogie boiler wagons and as their name suggests they were built to carry commercial boilers. The first is of a GC 40 ton 'Boiler J' No. 509972 loaded with a large boiler from Galloways. The numbers of this type were 509972 to 509974. The GN also had a pair of 'Boiler Ds' as depicted in plate 223, numbers 405747 and 405764.

Plate 223

Plate 222

103

Plate 224

Plate 225

Another way of carrying boilers was on twin wagons and plate 224 shows a GN 'Twin Boiler-D' capable of carrying 15 tons on each six wheeled wagon. The bolsters were shaped to receive a round load, but make up pieces were also provided. No. 438124 and 438123 were built by Messrs. Hurst Nelson Co. Ltd., of Motherwell in 1901 and was one of five pairs.

Similar to the flat wagons were the armour plate wagons owned by the GC of which there were ten types, three on 6 wheels and the remainder bogie vehicles. Plate 225 is of an 'Arm J' measuring 25 foot over the headstocks. It is seen here loaded with a heavy intricate steel casting made by the English Steel Corporation Ltd. Note the Spencer Moulton buffers, safety chains to the bogies, heavy axle boxes and the two screw hand brakes on the solebar.

GN/LNER 50 TON BOGIE 'BRICK' WAGON

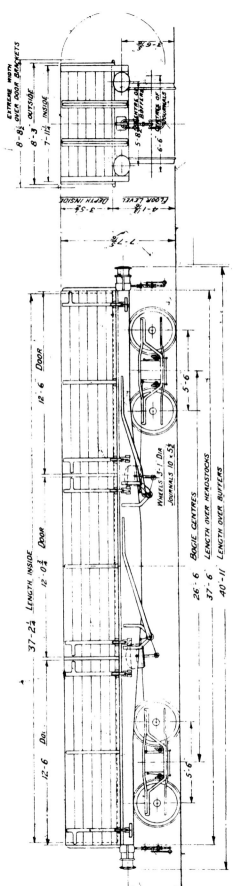

Figure 57

To convey the products of the London Brick Company's works at Fletton near Peterborough to the metropolis the GN introduced in 1921 twentyfive fully fitted 50 ton bogie brick wagons. These were often placed immediately behind the locomotive, thereby affording increased braking power. Built by the Leeds Forge Co. Ltd., they were numbered between 51001 and 51025, these being increased to 451001 to 451025 after 1923. A further twentyfive were added by the LNER in 1930 and numbered 163535 to 163559.

Almost identical in design, the only difference seems to have been in the buffers. The initial batch were as illustrated in plate 226, with oval heads and long fillets to the housing, while the second batch had 18 inch diameter heads and revised details of the casting.

Figure 57 is the GN diagram for the brick wagon and plate 226 depicts No. 51002 in GN livery when new.

Plate 226

Plate 227

Plate 228

Plate 227 is of another GN wagon photographed at Doncaster in 1925, by which time it had been renumbered 451004 and lettered in the LNER's style; while plate 228 illustrates the LNER version of the wagon, in this case the first of the batch No. 163535. Note the brake pipe, double brake levers and pressed steel components. Brick wagons were painted red oxide throughout their lives.

Less well known, but more numerous, were the 50 ton bogie 'Sulphate' wagons, of which 80 were built, numbered 164785 to 164864 to carry sulphate of ammonia from the ICI factory at Billingham. Mainly of steel construction, timber was however used for the doors. Plate 229 is of No. 164852 in wintry conditions.

Plate 229

Plate 230

The LNER took over seventeen of the 6 ton 'Powder Bs' depicted in plate 230 and only one remained by the end of 1947. No. 20064 was photographed at Kings Cross circa 1936 and plate 231 is a close up of the axleguard. Note the wooden brake block retained on these vans long after their replacement elsewhere. Presumably the risk of sparks from cast iron blocks was thought to be greater than the wooden ones catching alight. Figure 58 is LNER diagram 22 for a 7 ton 'Powder J' of standard Railway Clearing House design. LNER numbers were 147507 to 147511 built around 1928 and 260928 to 260947 of later construction.

Plate 231

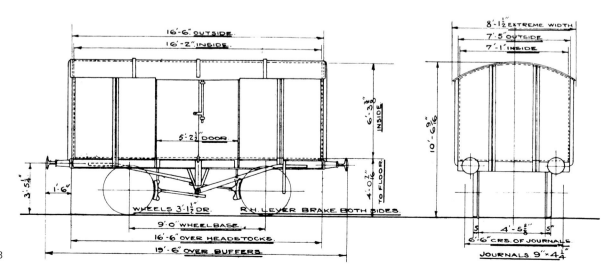

Figure 58

Plate 232

Plate 232 shows an NB 7 ton gunpowder van, No. 65410 built by Renishaw in 1904, in its pregrouping livery. These vans were coded 'Powder D' by the LNER and had 700000 added to their numbers. This particular van was withdrawn in November 1946, but twenty one others remained at nationalisation. Note the instructions on the doors.

The 9 ton 'Miser' wagons were unique to the GN and were used to carry gas economisers from the works of E. Green & Son Ltd. of Wakefield. There were two varieties of 15 and 16 feet over headstocks and the first batch had sides up until 1909 when they were removed. Painted white in pregrouping days they became grey under the LNER's jurisdiction. Plate 233 is of No. 435349.

Plate 233

Figure 59

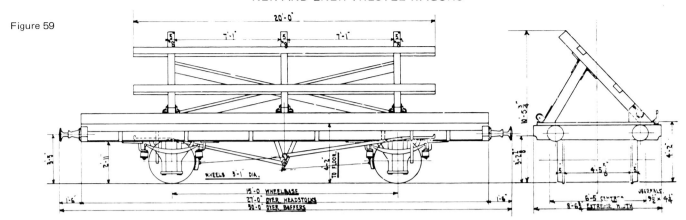

For carrying wide steel plates certain wagons were equipped with trestles so that the width of the plate was in a diagonal direction across the loading gauge. Figure 59 is NER diagram E 17 of a 12 ton 'Trestle B' converted from a plate wagon, while plate 234 shows a 40 ton 'Trestle G' made from a 'Quint C' also of NER origin.

Wider plates still could be conveyed, if a well wagon was used and plate 235 illustrates an LNER 40 ton 'Trestrol A' No. 203891 built in 1937. Other numbers were 203889 to 203896, 217296, 217297 and 217308 to 217313. This wagon has LMS axle box covers and other LMS features, such as the Simplex brake on the bogie, suggesting that like the 'Flat T' it is another joint venture. LMS vehicles were numbered 700300 to 700307 and 700312 to 700317.

Plate 234

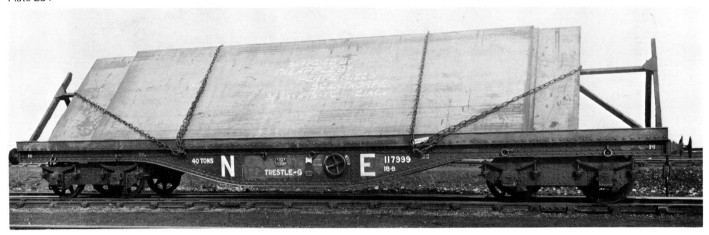

Plate 235

Plate 236

Plate 237

As their name implies well glass wagons were designed to carry plate glass and have a well through which the cased glass may be lowered to afford clearance beneath overline structures for tall loads. Plates 236 and 237 are of two types of GN 8 ton wagons with grease axle boxes, coded 'Glass G' and 'Glass C' respectively. The 'Glass G' design is of conventional design built in 1898, while the 'Glass C' has a pole down the centre to which the load may be secured and the end doors fold open to assist loading. There was only one 'Glass G', but two other 'Glass Cs' were numbered 400391 and 418675.

Plate 238 shows an NB 30 ton bogie 'Glass M' built in 1911, in pregrouping livery. It and one other like it were numbered 716306 and 716307 on the LNER, both lasting into BR days.

Plate 238

'PULLEY' WAGONS

Plate 239

Plate 240

Another awkward load to carry requiring special wagons were large wheels and pulleys. There were two GN 9 ton 'Pulley Bs' No. 415480 and 415481 of which the first is to be seen in plate 239. The GN also had a 12 ton version known by the LNER as a 'Pulley E' and numbered 446479 illustrated in plate 240. Both types were extinct before 1941.

An NB 15 ton pulley wagon built in 1900 and withdrawn in May 1947 is depicted in plate 241 of this wagon in 1923 recently painted in LNER livery and later coded 'Pulley G'. On the 'Pulleys E' and 'G' the cross members could be threaded through the spokes of the wheel thereby supporting it during its journey.

Plate 241

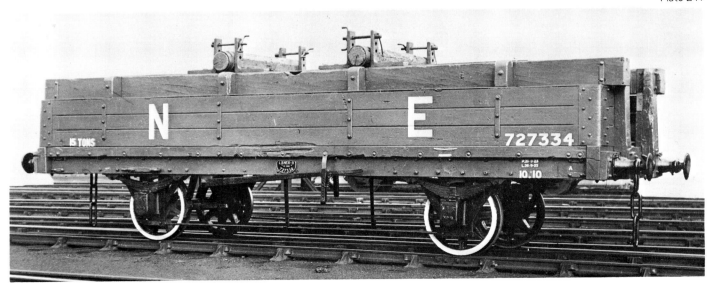

Plate 242

The NER had some six wheeled 32 ton and 40 ton flat wagons, 21 foot 2 inch over the headstock, 'Flat O' and 'Flat P', which could be equipped with special cradles for carrying large naval guns. In addition the 'Flat Ps' could be equipped with pivoted bolsters for carrying a pair of long girders between two wagons, as seen in plate 242 of Nos. 27284 and 69323 made up as a 66 ton 'Transformer A'. In 1929 the girders were remounted on two GC 55 ton bogie armour plate wagons, capable of carrying 70 tons, numbered 158253 and no doubt giving it a greater route availability. A similar set was also made and numbered 158356. Transformers were conveyed to various parts of the country from Trafford Park, Walthamstow and Newcastle on Tyne.

With the gathering of war clouds in 1938 the LNER built two 140 ton 'Gunsets' for 14 and 16 inch guns, which again seem to have been based on GC bogies. Plates 243 and 244 depict No. 231273 when new. The breech end of the gun would be placed on the swivelling cradle in the well, while the muzzle rested on the smaller cradle on the flat wagon No. 158253 from the 'Transformer A' set. The distance between the well and flat wagons was adjustable to take account of the two sizes of gun that could be carried. The second set was numbered 231274.

Plate 243

Plate 244

FLATROLS

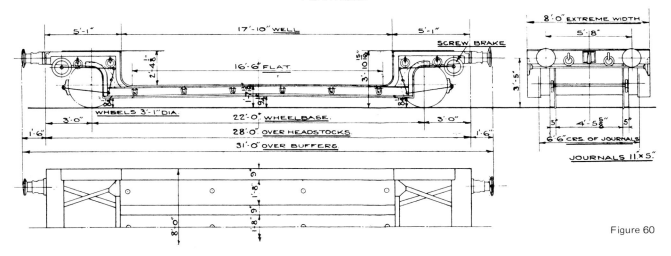

Figure 60

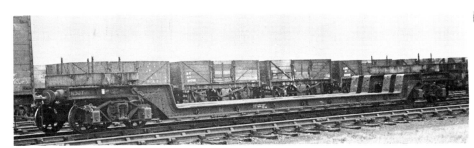

Plate 245

Plate 246

There were basically two types of trolley wagon, the 'Flatrol' which as its name suggests has a flat floor and the 'Weltrol' and 'Protrol' where the load is carried between the main side members. The four wheeled trolley is represented by figure 60 of diagram 42 for a 'Flatrol J', of which there were two Nos. 5499 and 4672. The GC built several examples of long bogie flat trolleys and plate 245 shows the sole example of a 30 ton 'Flatrol L' No. 538460. A short NER 35 ton 'Flatrol M' No. 77823 loaded with an 'out of gauge' boiler is illustrated in plate 246. The GN had two 40 ton 'Flatrol Ss' Nos. 415296 and 446478, of which the latter built in 1907 is to be seen in plate 247.

Plate 247

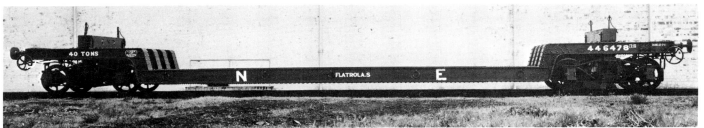

FLATROLS

SCREW BRAKE

10'-6"   5'-0"   5'-6"   1'-6½"

34'-6" WELL

32'-0" FLAT.

45'-6" CENTRES OF BOGIES.

55'-6" OVER HEADSTOCKS.

58'-7" OVER BUFFERS.

WHEELS 2'-9" DIA.

2'-3"

10'-6"   5'-6"   5'-0"   1'-6½"

8'-0" EXTREME WIDTH

7'-5"   5'-8½"   WELL

3'-5½"   4'-1½"

5"   4'-5⅝"

6'-9" CRS. OF JOURNALS.

13" x 7" JOURNALS.

Figure 61

Figure 61 is of diagram 32 for a 50 ton 'Flatrol Z'. The first No. 542483 was built by the GC in 1912 and another was added by the LNER in 1926 and given the number 147515. Later still No. 217321 was constructed and BR made six more. The GC diagram shows that these wagons were equipped with two logs measuring 16 inch square by 50 foot long and resting on a pair of 8 foot long 13 inch square bolsters over each bogie. These logs could be used to assist in supporting the load, but were optional.

In plate 248 there is a real monster, a 120 ton twenty four wheeled 'Flatrol AA'. Two pairs of six wheeled bogies each support a subframe, which in turn carries the main well structure. There was of course only one of these costly vehicles, No. 235318 built circa 1939.

Plate 248

LNER 20 TON 'FLATROL DD'

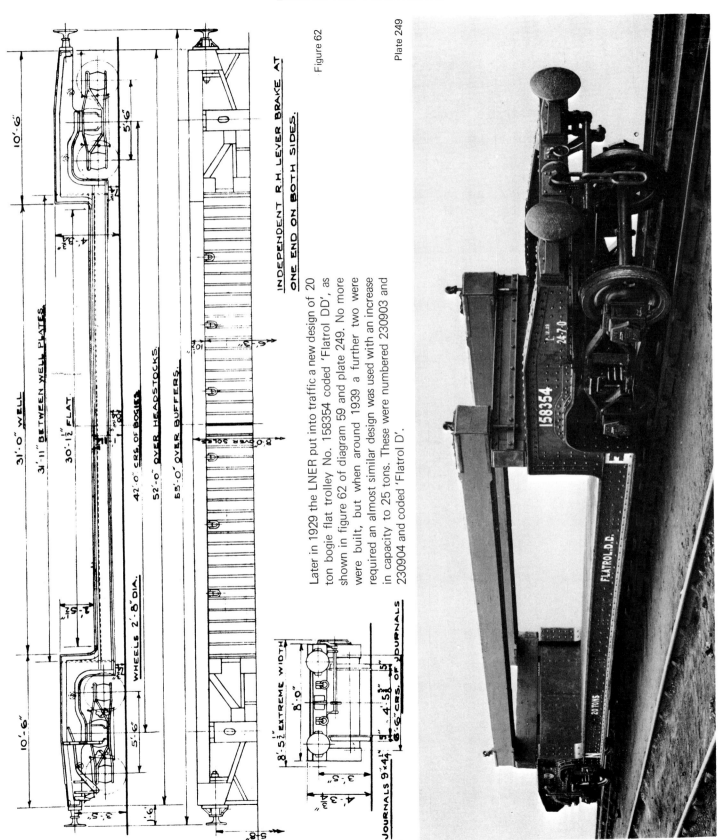

Figure 62

Plate 249

INDEPENDENT R.H. LEVER BRAKE AT
ONE END ON BOTH SIDES.

Later in 1929 the LNER put into traffic a new design of 20 ton bogie flat trolley No. 158354 coded 'Flatrol DD', as shown in figure 62 of diagram 59 and plate 249. No more were built, but when around 1939 a further two were required an almost similar design was used with an increase in capacity to 25 tons. These were numbered 230903 and 230904 and coded 'Flatrol D'.

115

WELTROLS

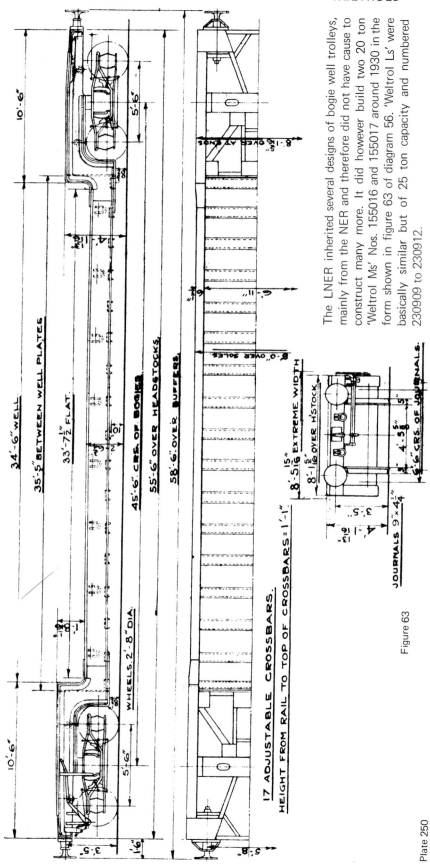

Figure 63

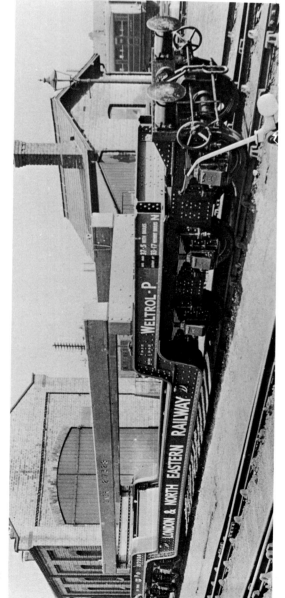

Plate 250

The LNER inherited several designs of bogie well trolleys, mainly from the NER and therefore did not have cause to construct many more. It did however build two 20 ton 'Weltrol Ms' Nos. 155016 and 155017 around 1930 in the form shown in figure 63 of diagram 56. 'Weltrol Ls' were basically similar but of 25 ton capacity and numbered 230909 to 230912.

In 1938 ten 50 ton 6 wheeled bogie well trolleys were built, as depicted in plate 250 of No. 217328, of which five were allocated to the LNER, the other numbers being 217304 to 217307, and five to the LMS, who numbered theirs 700333, 700337 to 700340.

Plate 251

Similar to 'Weltrols' were the 'Protrols'. Whereas the first usually had adjustable crossbars between the bottom flanges of the main well girders, the 'Protrol' had fixed cross and longitudinal members on the two centre lines of the vehicle. They were therefore especially useful for the conveyance of ships' propellors.

Plate 251 is of an NB 25 ton 'Protrol E' built by Messrs. Hurst Nelson in 1921. Seen here as No. 36919 when new it was renumbered 736919 by the LNER. Of similar size but greater capacity is the NER 40 ton 'Protrol F' built in 1911. Note the inside bearings to the wheels and spoked hand brakes on the outside ends of the bogies. Both were the sole examples of their class and lasted until nationalisation.

Plate 252

Plate 253

Plate 254

Plate 253 is of a medium sized 10 ton cattle wagon built in 1924 to a NER design and plate 254 shows a similar wagon No. 57394 equipped with AVB and through steam pipe. Cattle trucks were graded according to the inside length with large at 18 foot, medium at 15 ft. 6 in. and small only 13 ft. 6 in.: although few if any of the small size came into LNER stock. Cattle wagons should always be marshalled next to the engine to afford a smooth ride for the livestock and, if brake fitted, provide additional braking power.

Plate 255

Plate 256

By grouping the GN only had large cattle wagons and these were equipped with a movable partition which could be set to provide small, medium or large accommodation. Plate 255 illustrates an 18 ft. 2½ in. long vehicle built in 1891 with four end posts similar to the GN vans on page 27. Note the round push rod to the solitary brake shoe and the long springs. The later design of GN cattle truck had only two end stanchions and was 19 foot long. The example in plate 256 was built in 1914, while plate 257 is of No. 410805 loaded and with the partition in the 'small' position. The destination chalked above the load reads 'Grantham'. Note that the roof is without any canvas or felt protection. All the wagons on this page are of 6 ton capacity and equipped with through vacuum pipes, screw couplings and oil lubricated axle boxes. They also have doors of the falling type and two removable bars in the upper portion of the door opening.

Plate 257

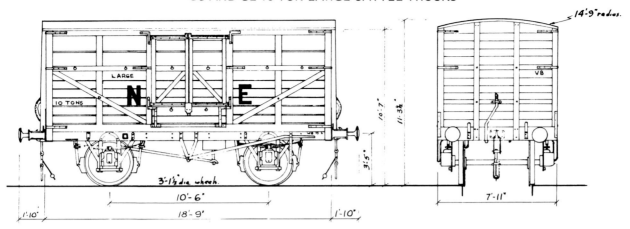

Figure 64   Plate 258

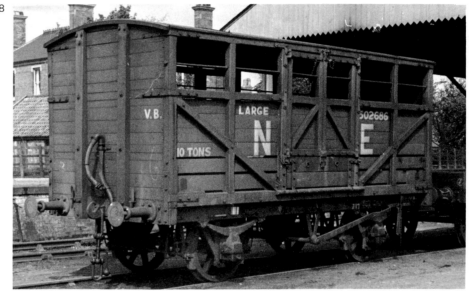

Figure 64 and plate 258 are of a GC 10 ton large cattle wagon equipped with AVB. The door way in this design had a pair of side hung doors reaching to the cantrail and a two plank falling flap. The photograph was taken at Newark circa. 1938.

Plate 259 depicts a GE 10 ton 18 ft. 7 in. long large non-fitted cattle wagon built in 1910 with diagonal cross bracing to the side panels.

Plate 259

120

Plate 260

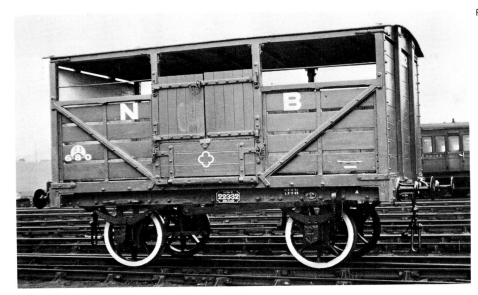

In plates 260 and 261 there are two versions of the NB 8 ton cattle wagon. The first has a wooden underframe, grease axle boxes and wooden end posts. The figure '23' in the crescent almost certainly indicates the year of overhaul and not its building date. However, it is interesting to note that pregrouping livery was still being applied in September, 1923. Plate 261 is of a steel framed version built in 1914 with oil lubrication. Figure 65 is a drawing for a GNS 6 ton cattle truck. Note the 3 ft. 7 in. diameter spoked wheels. Up until grouping all the Scottish companies had standardised on the medium size of cattle wagon.

Plate 261

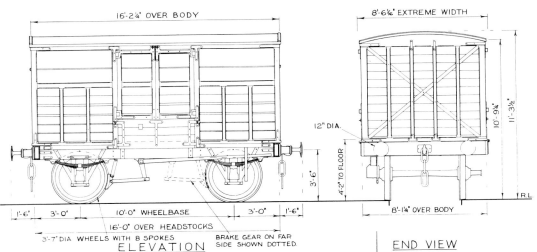

Figure 65

ELEVATION

END VIEW

LNER 10 TON LARGE CATTLE TRUCKS

Plate 262

All LNER standard cattle wagons were of the large size, usually with a 9 foot wheelbase and both automatic brake fitted and non-fitted versions were produced. The latter is shown in plate 262 of No. 150878 built at Doncaster in 1927. Note that, although equipped with only hand brake, screw couplings are fitted.

Figure 66 and plate 263 illustrate the AVB version with through steam pipe as well to permit working in passenger trains. Plate 263 taken after the war shows No. 150927 with the 'down at the heel look' indicative of a weak underframe. It also has open fronted axle boxes, which were almost certainly fitted sometime after building.

Plate 263

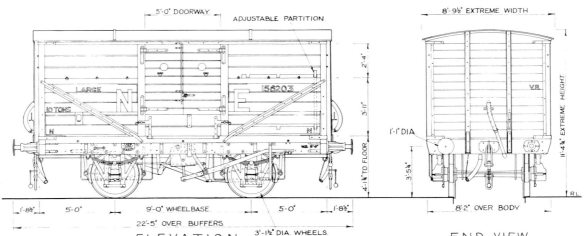

Figure 66

ELEVATION

END VIEW

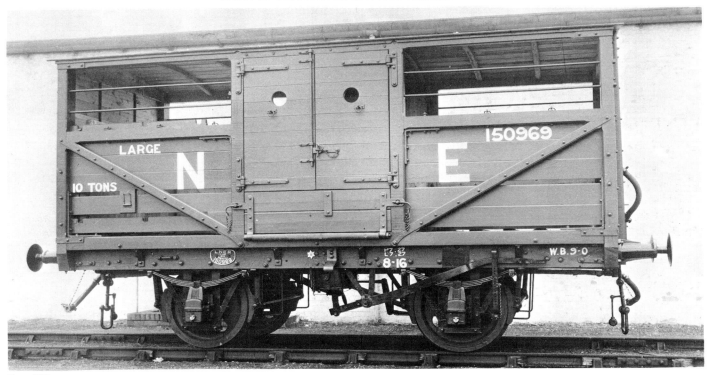

Plate 264

Plate 264 is another view of a 9 foot wheelbase AVB fitted cattle wagon, while plate 265 shows one of the rare examples with a 10 foot wheelbase. About a dozen were converted to the increased dimension and seven built new as such: but by 1937 when this photograph was taken cattle traffic had dropped so dramatically that no more cattle trucks were built by the LNER and surplus fitted vehicles were converted to 'Conflat Vs', as described on page 69.

Plate 265

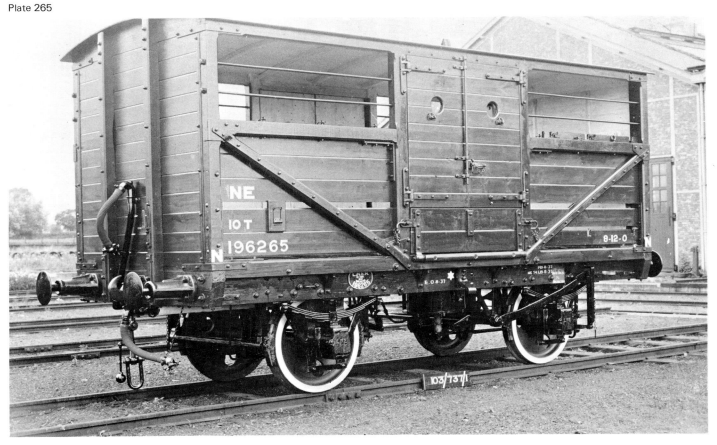

Plate 266

With cattle wagons dealt with our survey of traffic wagons is complete and it is time to turn to non-revenue earning vehicles. First the loco coal wagon, which as its name suggests was used to convey coal for locomotive purposes from the pithead to the engine sheds. In this respect many loco coal wagons were nothing more than ordinary mineral wagons set aside for this specific purpose and indeed many an elderly open wagon eked out its days on such duties.

Although specially designed in 1906 as a loco coal wagon, the NER's 20 ton wagons to diagram Q2, as illustrated in plate 266, clearly had a family likeness to that company's hopper coal wagons described on page 59. However, they were not equipped with hoppers and two pairs of side hung doors were provided one each side instead. This wagon was photographed at Shildon when new in 1915. The initials 'S D' painted on the sides between the doors stand for the Southern Division of the NER. Plate 267 shows a H & B 15 ton 9 plank 18 foot long loco coal wagon at Kings Cross around 1936. This also has twin doors, but this time of the falling type. Plate 268 is a detail of the axleguard etc. of a similar wagon.

Plate 267

Plate 268

Plate 269

If the railway companies were unable to persuade private wagon owners of the advantages to be gained from larger capacity wagons, when it came to the conveyance of coal for their own purposes they could call the tune. Soon after building the 15 ton mineral wagons described on pages 54 and 127, the GN introduced a 20 ton design with 9 planks which had bottom doors as well as a single door on each side. Subsequently the design was modified to one of 7 planks and twin doors of the falling type, as depicted in plate 269 and figure 67. The earlier wagons were rebuilt and a variety of details can be found between wagons of this group. 300 wagons of this type were taken over by the LNER.

Figure 67

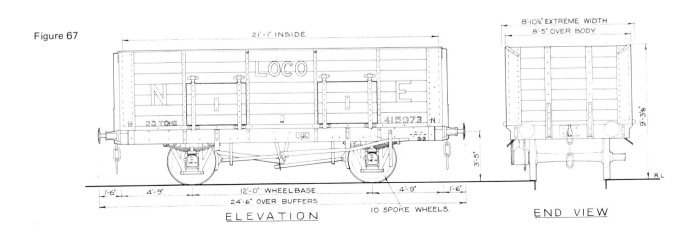

ELEVATION

END VIEW

Plate 270

After the first World War the GN had some 12 ton 7 plank 16 ft. 5½ in. long loco coal wagons built by contractors and an example is illustrated in plate 270 of No. 454941 built in 1921. It is equipped with oil lubricated axleboxes by Messrs. Harrison and Camm Ltd., of Rotherham the covers of which are also inscribed 'W↓D'.

The GC 10 ton 6 plank end door loco coal wagon was photographed sometime after October 1930 and, as can be seen, it still wears its GC livery. The wagon was built in 1901 probably by Messrs. Sam E. Stevens of Doncaster, whose axleboxes it carries and who certainly seemed to have repaired it a couple of times. Note the sprag in the left hand wheel.

Plate 271

Plate 272

Plate 273

The pair of 8 plank loco coal wagons seen in plate 272 are, on the left, a GE 12 ton end door 15 ft. 11 in. over headstocks and the other is a GN 15 ton.

A smaller GE loco coal wagon is to be seen in plate 273 of an 8 ton 7 plank on steel underframe built in 1897.

The GE also produced a 20 ton loco coal wagon, but this time of all steel construction, one of which is shown in plate 274 of No. 600125 built in 1903. Observe the two positions for the word 'LOCO' on these wagons and the note 'This wagon to be returned to Temple Mills Shops Oct 1937' on the 20 ton.

Plate 274

Plate 275

Plate 275 is of a GNS 10 ton 5 plank 16 foot long open wagon No. 803755 built at Inverurie in 1908 seen here in service as a loco coal wagon at New England in July 1952. Evidently still in LNER livery, but noted by the photographer, as being painted black. Note the steel underframe, grease axle boxes, large diameter spoked wheels and simple brake gear on this photograph and plate 276 of a similar wagon No. 803772 at Colwick in 1936. First batches of LNER loco coal wagons were of the type shown in plate 277 of 20 ton capacity, with end and bottom doors as well as twin flap doors in the sides. No. 30987 was constructed in 1928.

Plate 277

Plate 276

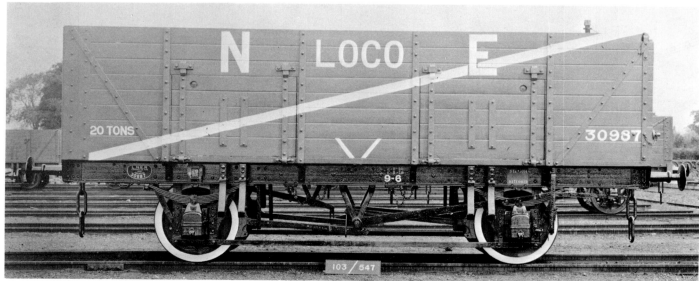

LNER 20 TON 8 PLANK LOCO COAL WAGONS

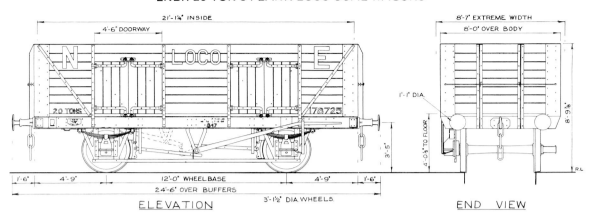

Figure 68

ELEVATION

END VIEW

Figure 68 and plates 278 and 279 show the subsequent and more common LNER design of 20 ton 8 plank loco coal wagon with two pairs of side hung doors in each side. No. 231030 in plate 279 was built in 1939. Split axleboxes and spoked wheels were fitted to earlier wagons, these being changed respectively to open front and three hole later as illustrated.

Plate 278

Plate 279

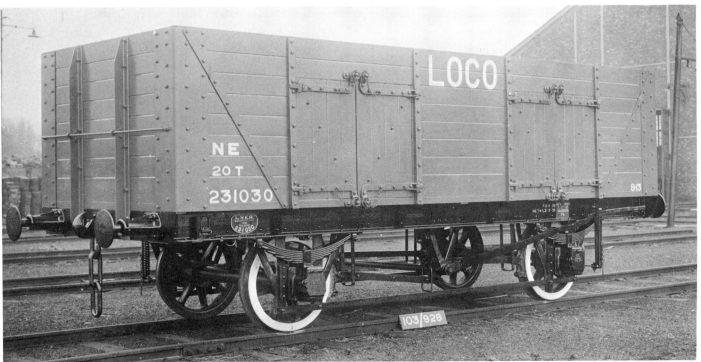

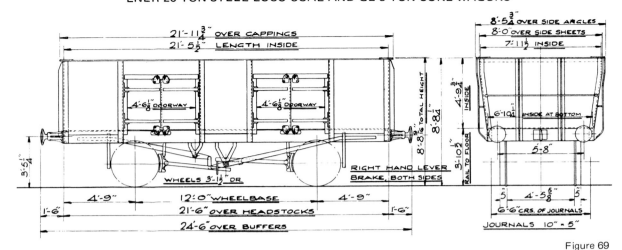

Figure 69

Plate 280

In 1935 a batch of 100 all steel 20 ton loco coal wagons were produced by Metro Cammell as depicted in plate 280 and incorporated various pressed steel fittings. Further batches were put in hand later until by December 1947 there were 499. Another design is shown in figure 69 of Diagram 125 of which 180 were made.

For the conveyance of coke GE 8 ton 7 plank wagons were used. No. 601029, seen at Stratford in plate 281, was built late in the last century and has 'Empty to Beckton' painted on it.

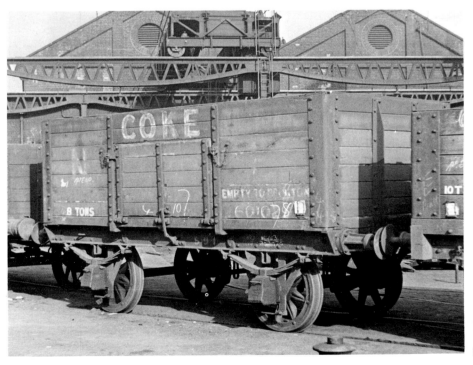

Plate 281

Plate 282

The Civil Engineer's Department of any railway operated a considerable number of wagons in connection with the maintenance and renewal of the permanent way and construction and repair of other engineering features and buildings. Many of these wagons tended to be cast offs from the Traffic Department, no longer fit for revenue earning service, and lingering on long after others of its class had been scrapped and frequently becoming decrepit to a degree.

However, the two GN 8 ton 2 plank dropside wagons illustrated in plates 282 and 283 were probably purpose built at Doncaster in 1888 and 1901 respectively. Note the door stops and canvas flaps over the axle boxes to prevent the ingress of ballast. The first has a left handed brake lever on the near side.

Plate 283

Plate 284

Plate 285

To transport 45 foot rails, a pair of 22 ft. 9½ in. long 2 plank dropside wagons each equipped with a bolster and pins were used. In this form each wagon was permitted to carry a load of 10 tons. Alternatively 12 tons of ballast could be conveyed: a drop end being provided at one end of the wagon only to allow the rails to pass through, as shown in plate 286.

The contrasting hues of Engineers' blue can be seen by comparing plates 284 and 285. The numbers suffixed 'E' were renumbered in the 470xxx series sometime after grouping, later to be altered again to 94xxxx. Plates 284 and 286 were taken at Kings Cross around 1938.

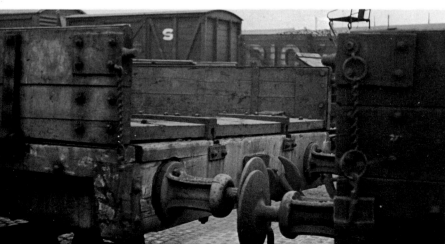

Plate 286

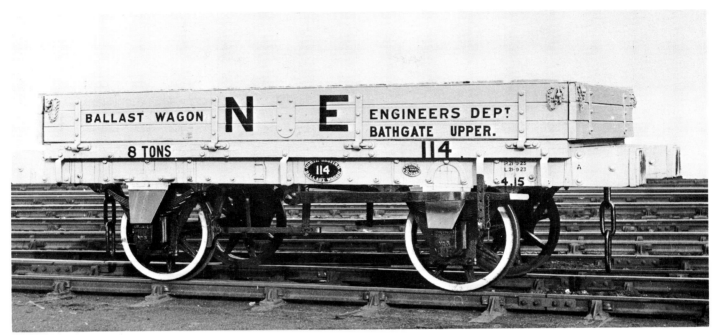

Plate 287

Although dumb buffers had been eliminated from revenue earning stock even in Scotland prior to 1922, as plate 287 demonstrates the NB passed on to the LNER some ballast wagons so equipped. The 8 ton 3 plank dropside No. 114 was built at Cowlairs in 1897. The very pale shade of blue and dark lettering, together with the metal covers to the grease axleboxes should be noticed.

Most of the Midland and Great Northern's wagon stock was split up between the LNER and LMS, but service vehicles and brake vans were retained. Plate 288 shows a 2 plank dropside No. 116 with rounded ends loaded with what can only be described as firewood.

Plate 288

Plate 289

Plate 290

Some wagons specially built for the Engineer's Department were the 25 ton steel ballast hoppers depicted in plates 289 and 291, which show each side of No. 843E built by the Leeds Forge Co. Ltd., in 1926. The design was by the wagon contractor and the LMS received some exactly similar, except for the provision of three link couplings and associated shorter buffers.

There were three hopper doors in the bottom operated by the wheels at the platform end. As the train was slowly drawn forward, the outer doors discharged in the cess or 'six foot' either side of the track and the centre one into the 'four foot'. The ballast was then spread by the ballast plough brakes shown on page 142.

Plate 291

LNER 25 TON STEEL BALLAST HOPPERS

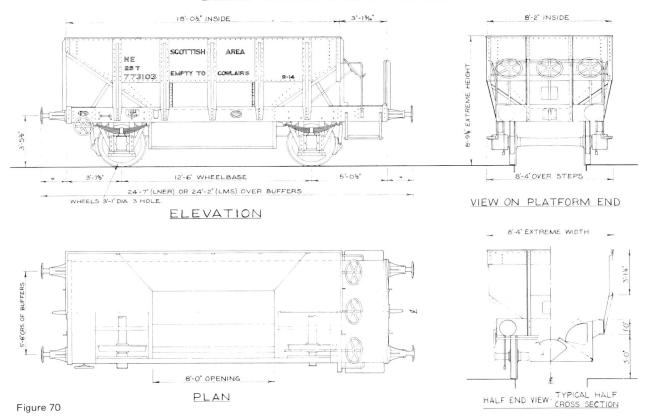

Figure 70

ELEVATION

VIEW ON PLATFORM END

PLAN

HALF END VIEW · TYPICAL HALF CROSS SECTION

Figure 70 is a drawing for the 25 ton steel ballast hopper and plates 290, 292 and 293 show details of the brake rigging, inside of the hopper and end platform respectively of a hopper actually built in 1949 and still at work in August 1972 at Inverness.

Other numbers were 163504 supplied in 1930 (North Eastern Area, empty to Lackenby Slag Plant), 163522 and 163525 also built in 1930 and 773103 constructed in 1937 (Scottish Area, empty to Cowlairs).

Plate 292

Plate 293

Plate 294

The GN 9 ton sleeper wagon depicted in plate 294 appears to be a conversion from the 4 plank open wagon described on page 13, having had an additional plank fitted to raise the sides. While the wagon in plate 295 seems to be a redundant GN 9 ton 7 plank coal wagon.

Plate 295

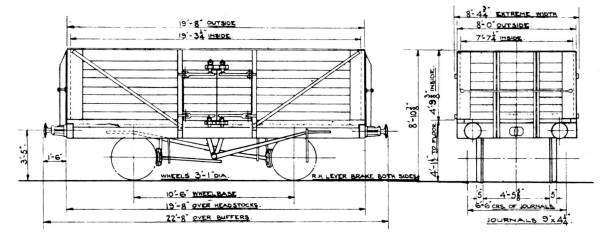

Figure 71

Plate 296

Figure 71 and plates 296 and 297 all show the LNER 12 ton 8 plank sleeper wagons on wooden underframes. There was also a design on a steel underframe. No. 154906 was built in 1929 and No. 216855 in 1938. Note the side hung doors. Sleeper wagons were painted wagon grey.

Plate 297

GN 30 TON SLEEPER WAGONS

Plate 298

Plate 299

Plate 300

Plate 298 shows a GN 10 ton 3 plank dropside sleeper wagon built at Doncaster in 1899. The wagon is mounted on four rigid axles with the outer and inner ones kept as close as possible in an effort to minimise difficulties when rounding curves.

Plate 300 illustrates one of two GN 30 ton bogie sleeper wagons 38 ft. 6 in. long constructed in 1908. The sides have been divided into two for ease of raising. Plate 299 is a detail of the bogie to No. 470069 of a slightly longer vehicle at Kings Cross about 1937.

The origin of the 40 ton bogie wagon No. 421E in plate 301 is not clear, but as well as the GNR number plate, illustrated in plate 4, it has other GN features such as the bogie and buffers. It has been altered at some time for use in the Morris track relayer train and was photographed at York in 1972.

Plate 301

Bogie vehicles for carrying primarily rails, but also sleepers and ballast, were developed by the LNER and figure 72 shows an early design suitable for 45 foot rails.

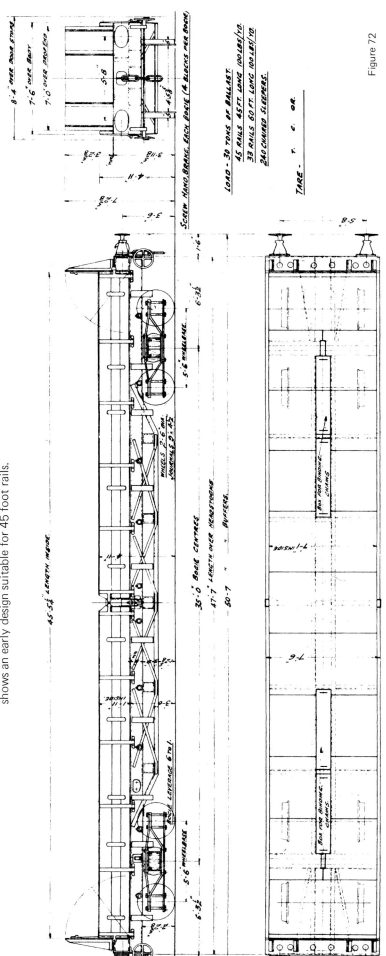

Figure 72

LOAD - 30 TONS OF BALLAST:
45 RAILS 45 FT. LONG 100 LBS/YD.
33 RAILS 60 FT. LONG 100 LBS/YD.
240 CHAIRED SLEEPERS.

SCREW HAND BRAKE EACH BOGIE (4 BLOCKS PER BOGIE)

TARE - T. C. QR.

Plate 302

Plate 303

To cope with the increase of rail length to 60 feet, new bogie rail wagons were made about 65 feet over headstocks and of 40 ton capacity. Small diameter wheels were used to enable the floor to be kept as low as practical, thereby easing the task of loading rails by hand. Plates 303 and 304 illustrate bogie and end details of the more usual 40 ton rail wagon with the reversed channel solebar and angle truss underframe. Under BR these were coded 'Dolphin' and some had the sides stripped off so that they could be loaded with pre-fabricated track panels. Note the rectangular buffer heads, screw brake, door stops and pins to retain a load of rails.

Further 40 ton bogie rail wagons were obtained in the mid 1930s by converting redundant 64 ft. 5¾ in. long wagons from the Morris track relayer train of which No. 633451 in plate 302 is an example with a plate girder underframe.

Plate 304

NER AND GN 10 TON BALLAST BRAKES

Figure 73

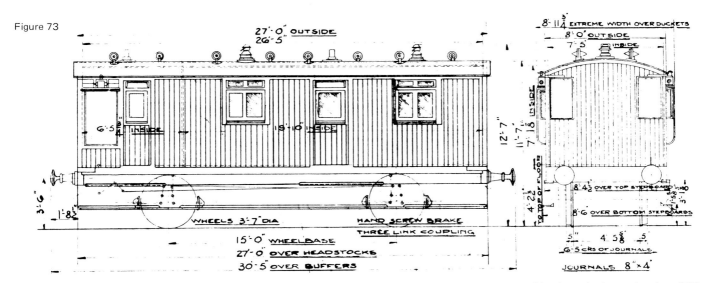

The Engineer's brake vans were often longer than normal, additional space being taken up by accommodation for the platelayers or surfacement required to accompany the ballast train and carry out work in section. Figure 73 is of a NER 10 ton ballast brake, but the diagram, No. 35, is also to be found in the LNER book and may be for the two additional vans to the same design built in 1925 for use on the Northern Scottish Area.

A GN example with a roof lookout is shown in plate 305 of No. 42E constructed at Doncaster in 1901. Note the three doors, in addition to the guard's, giving access to crude compartments for the platelayers. Both these vans were clearly purpose made, but many brake vans redundant from traffic duties were converted to ballast brakes, usually by boarding up the verandahs and doorways at one end.

Plate 305

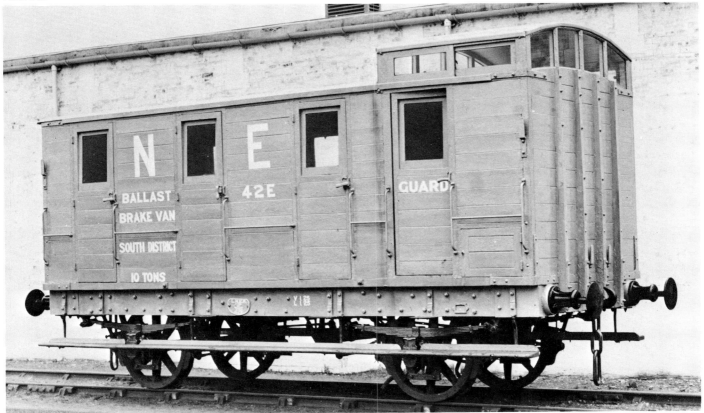

141

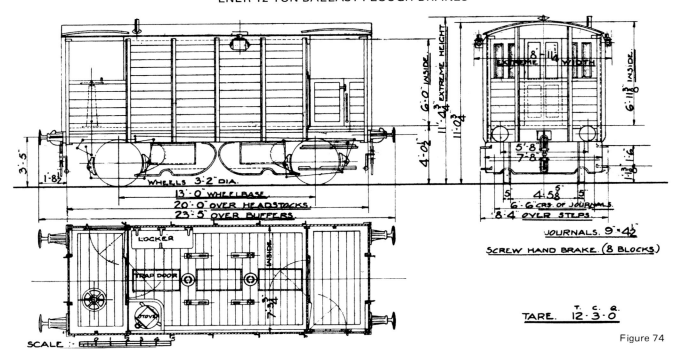

Figure 74

Figure 74 and plate 306 are of the LNER 12 ton ballast plough brake vans used in conjunction with the 25 ton steel ballast hoppers described on page 134. In the photograph the plough is in the raised position, but at the site of relay-ing it would be lowered and the train drawn along at slow speed to spread the ballast. No. 860E was built in 1926. Another was No. 163532 constructed by Metro-Cammell in 1930 and allocated to Lackenby Slag Plant.

Plate 306

Plate 307
The pretreatment of water for locomotive purposes in certain areas resulted in a white sludge which was collected in redundant locomotive tenders fitted out for the purpose. Plate 307 is of an old GN 6 wheeled tender at Offord in April 1952 and numbered 941626. Note the buffers and drawhook fitted at what was formerly the footplate end.

Another type of vehicle required by the locomotive department were wagons for the conveyance of sand. In plate 308 an ancient GE 10 ton 5 plank open wagon is seen allocated to this duty. Canvas sheets have been provided above the grease lubricated axleboxes in an attempt to protect them from the sand. Plate 308

Some idea of the heterogeneous collection of steam breakdown cranes taken over by the LNER at grouping can be gained by studying Appendix 5, which lists all these cranes together with those acquired between 1923 and 1947 with their allocations, where known.

Plate 309 is an example of the most numerous type, the Cowans Sheldon 15 ton with swan neck jib, in this case No. 981508 originally acquired by the NB in 1897 and seen here at Kittybrewster in 1949. The NER, GN and GC had similar cranes.

The GE was one of only two railway companies that attempted to design and build its own steam breakdown cranes and in their case these were highly successful, lasting until the mid '60s. Plate 310 shows one of the two 20 tonners built at Stratford in 1908. They were much ahead of their time in having hydraulic controls to the motions.

Plate 311 and figures 75 and 76 are of the 25 ton cranes made by Craven Bros. of Manchester for the NER in 1907. One of these has been put aside for preservation.

Plate 309

Plate 310

Plate 311

35 AND 45 TON STEAM BREAKDOWN CRANES

Plate 312

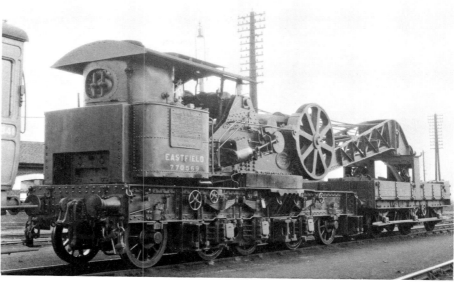

Liking the three Craven 25 ton cranes, the NER ordered two 35 ton cranes which were delivered in 1912. To carry the greater weight of the larger capacity cranes an additional axle was fitted thereby changing the wheel arrangement from 2-4-2 to 2-6-2. One of the two 35 ton cranes was requisitioned during the First World War and never returned. Although replaced by a crane of similar capacity, the order was fulfilled by Cowans, Sheldon. Plate 312 shows the remaining crane at Eastfield after it had been drafted to Scotland in the early days of the LNER. The GN had a similar crane which was transferred to the GC section about the same time.

To handle his new pacifics in the event of mishap, Gresley bought two 45 ton cranes from Cowans, Sheldon in 1926 and stationed them at the strategic centres of Doncaster and Gateshead. In plate 313 the latter's is seen arriving at Blaydon Carriage Sidings in 1939. Mounted on only two 4 wheeled bogies, the maximum axle load was 21 tons, which must have somewhat limited their route availability.

Plate 313

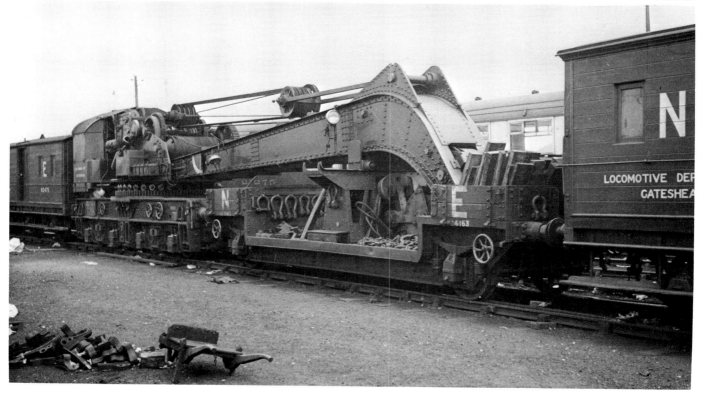

NER 25 TON CRAVEN STEAM BREAKDOWN CRANES

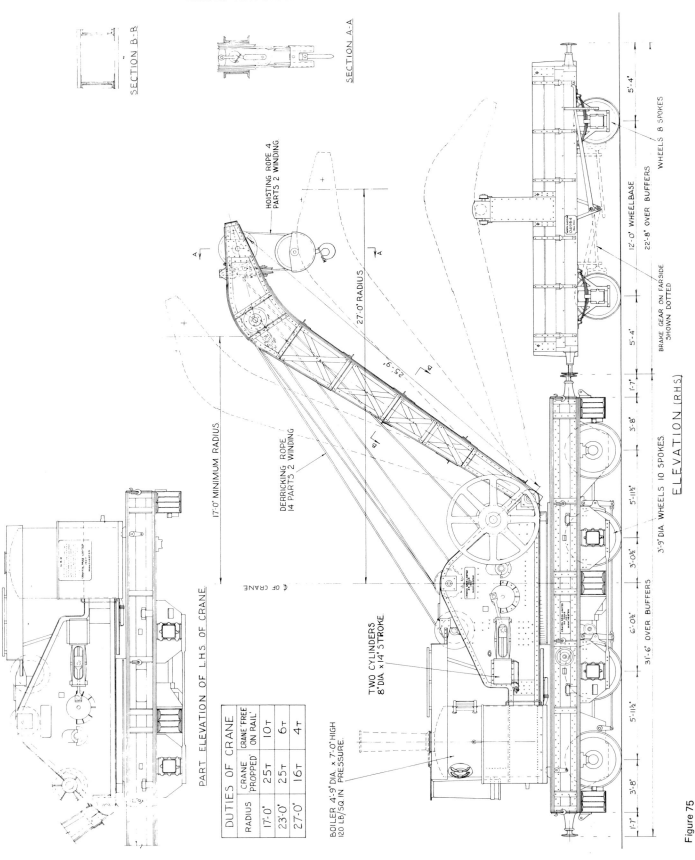

SECTION B-B

SECTION A-A

PART ELEVATION OF L.H.S. OF CRANE

HOISTING ROPE 4 PARTS 2 WINDING

27'-0" RADIUS

17'-0" MINIMUM RADIUS

25'-9"

DERRICKING ROPE 14 PARTS 2 WINDING

₵ OF CRANE

TWO CYLINDERS 8" DIA x 14" STROKE.

BOILER 4'-9" DIA x 7'-0" HIGH 120 LB/SQ IN PRESSURE.

DUTIES OF CRANE

RADIUS	CRANE PROPPED	CRANE 'FREE' ON RAIL
17'-0"	25т	10т
23'-0"	25т	6т
27'-0"	16т	4т

5'-4"

WHEELS 8 SPOKES

12'-0" WHEELBASE

22'-8" OVER BUFFERS

BRAKE GEAR ON FARSIDE SHOWN DOTTED

5'-4"

1'-7"

3'-8"

5'-11½"

3'-9" DIA WHEELS 10 SPOKES

3'-0½"

6'-0½"

31'-6" OVER BUFFERS

5'-11½"

3'-8"

1'-7"

ELEVATION (R.H.S.)

Figure 75

146

NER 25 TON CRAVEN STEAM BREAKDOWN CRANES

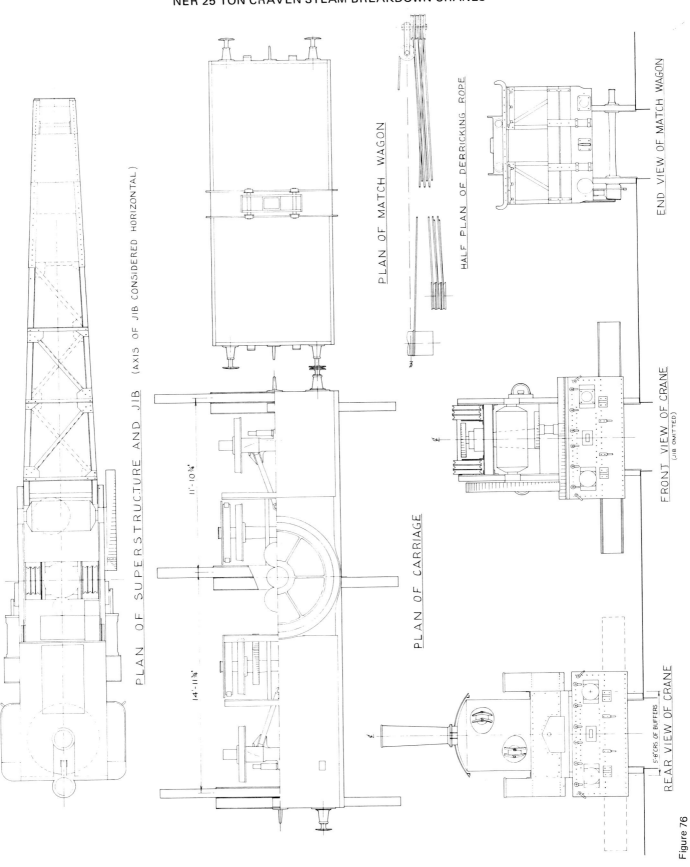

PLAN OF SUPERSTRUCTURE AND JIB (AXIS OF JIB CONSIDERED HORIZONTAL)

PLAN OF MATCH WAGON

HALF PLAN OF DERRICKING ROPE

END VIEW OF MATCH WAGON

PLAN OF CARRIAGE

FRONT VIEW OF CRANE (JIB OMITTED)

REAR VIEW OF CRANE

5'-8" CRS OF BUFFERS

11'-10¾"

14'-11¾"

Figure 76

Plate 314

Plate 315

From late 1937 with war clouds gathering, British railways started to plan their air raid precautions. Among the many things put in hand was the ordering of a dozen 45 ton steam breakdown cranes to assist in dealing with the increase in emergencies along the line to be anticipated in the time of war. The LNER's allocation was six, all supplied by Cowans, Sheldon in 1940. Plate 314 shows the one sent to New England seen here in August 1952. Note the raised chimney, which would have to be lowered prior to travelling in train formation.

Some idea of the gearing necessary to drive the four motions of hoisting the hook, derricking the jib, slewing the superstructure and travelling the crane at walking pace along the track can be gained from plate 315. These cranes were designed to travel on all companies lines and to keep the axle loads down they were equipped at each end of the carriage with relieving bogies. As plate 316 demonstrates, one or both and the match wagon could be detached at the site of operations and shunted or lifted out of the way.

Plate 316

Plate 317

All breakdown trains included tool and mess vans. Plate 317 shows an old NB coach serving as mess van No. 971522 for Eastfield's crew at Stevenston in 1949. In plate 318 we have a GN 6 wheel brake van No. 43829 allocated to the West Riding District Loco Dept.

Plate 319 depicts a GC horse drawn fire engine by Metropolitan mounted on a 4 wheeled flat trolley wagon stationed at Annesley. A vertical boiler supplied steam to the cylinders which drove the water pump.

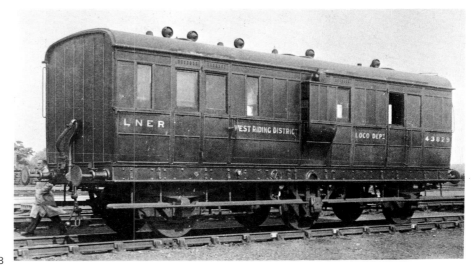

Plate 318

Plate 319

Plate 320

Plate 321

As well as steam breakdown cranes there were steam travelling cranes usually allocated to the Engineer's Department to carry out all the lifting associated with work on the track. Plate 320 is of a 10 ton Coles crane No. 773082 built in 1936 and its match wagon, No. 773083, probably converted from a 6 wheeled coach underframe. These were to be renumbered three years later 970096 and 970097 respectively. Plate 321 shows a sister crane for Ladybank No. 773080 with its jib raised and match wagon No. 773081, likewise renumbered 970094 and 970095.

Other crane builders supplied cranes for this type of work and plate 322 depicts No. 940212, a 10 ton Grafton constructed in 1937 and allocated to the District Engineer Kings Cross, but depoted at Hitchin, where it was photographed looking in need of a coat of paint in August 1952. Note that both cranes have lattice jibs and crude corrugated iron shelters for the boiler, machinery and the driver.

Plate 322

Plate 323   HAND CRANES

For much of the last century railway companies had to make do with hand cranes for breakdown and other lifting work. Plate 323 illustrates the breakdown train at Tyne Dock in early BR days and it includes a 12 ton hand crane built in 1892 for use on the NER. The mess and tool vans should be compared with those in plate 313.

Travelling hand cranes could be used at yards without fixed cranage for handling goods or railway materials. Plate 324 depicts No. 962108, a 5 ton crane allocated to the Goods Department of Cambridge District at St. Ives, Huntingdonshire in July 1953. The jib is in the raised position and the rail clips in place, suggesting that the crane had recently been in use.

Plate 324

TWIN GAS TANKS

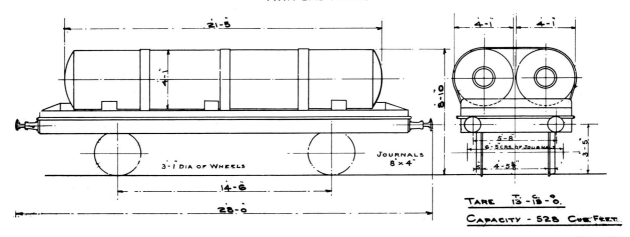

TARE 13 - 13 - 0.
CAPACITY - 528 CUB. FEET.

Figure 77

Plate 325

To supply the ever reducing number of gas light coaches, some dining cars and even stations the LNER maintained a small fleet of gas tanks. These usually consisted of tanks fitted to redundant 4 wheel carriage underframes, and if so, permitted to work in passenger trains. Figure 77 and plate 325 show a non-fitted NER example, the photograph being of No. 43075, while plate 326 is of a GN vehicle.

Plate 326

Plate 327

Single, twin and even triple tanks were used as plate 327 and figure 78 demonstrate. Note that the GN vehicles are equipped with automatic vacuum brake, through steam heating pipes, screw couplings and Maunsell wheel centres. Some GN built gasholder trucks were transferred to the Southern Scottish Area.

Figure 78

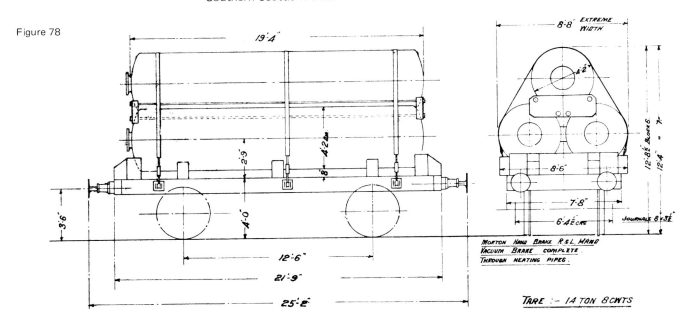

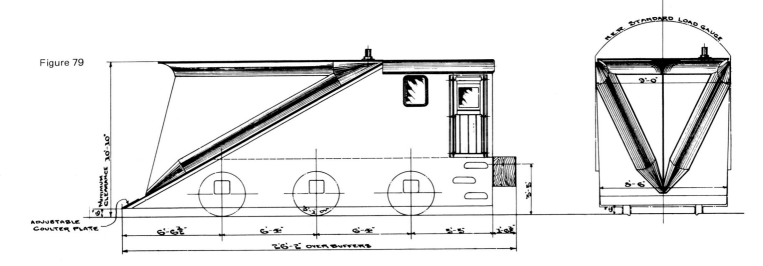

Figure 79

To deal with snow blocked lines the NER built some 6 wheeled independent snowploughs and figure 79 is a diagram for such a vehicle, some of which were still available for use in 1972.

Plate 328 shows a GN 7 ton clerestory van converted into a machine fitters van. Access will have been through a door positioned on the other side only.

Plate 328

Plate 329

A similar van of GC origin for the Telegraph Section is to be seen in plate 329. This was photographed at Finsbury Park circa. 1937. Note the small windows, the steps and cast iron letters and numerals screwed to backing boards.

As service vans became even older their movements were restricted to their home yards and for this reason were painted in the green livery. Nonetheless some lasted as stores vans and the like for very extended periods. Plate 330 shows No. 01759 an old NER 8 ton van with outside framing still at Tweedmouth engine shed in April 1966.

Others would be found in sidings around the main works and plate 331 is of two GE 7 ton vans at Stratford before the last war. However, unlike the previous vans these have oil axle boxes.

Plate 331

Plate 330

NER 10 TON BRAKE VANS

Plate 332

Despite the variety of wagons from all the four groups, as a result of the common user agreement, and private owners likely to be found in most goods trains, when it comes to the brake van this will almost certainly be from the home company. In pregrouping days, because of the distinctive designs adopted by the various railways, the goods brake van at the tail of a train was as much an indication of the operating territory as the engine pulling the train or the signal boxes passed on the way. After grouping the brakes of the constituent companies could and often did work all over the LNER system soon to be joined by standard designs.

Construction of the NER 10 ton brake vans shown in plates 332 and 333 and figure 80 continued after grouping. Many of the constructional features found their way into the LNER's first standard design. Note the early and later styles of lettering in plates 332 and 333 respectively.

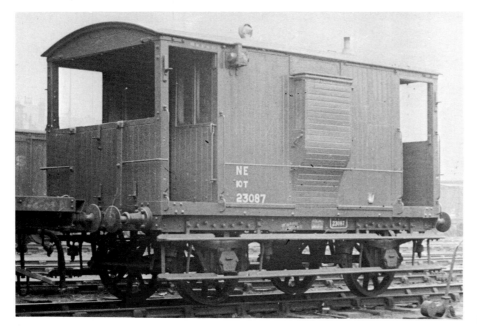

Plate 333

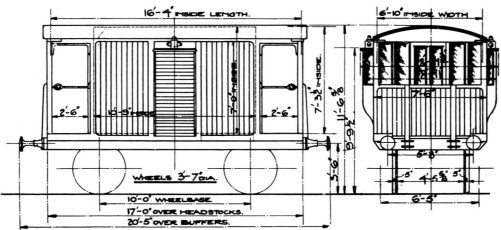

Figure 80

Figure 81

The Hull and Barnsley Railway's design of 20 ton brake van is depicted in figure 81. Doors were only provided at the right hand end on each side and the van was fitted with 'Iracier' axleboxes.

The GN had brake vans of various weights and wheel arrangements. In plate 334 is the 20 ton 8 wheeled brake in pregrouping livery. This also had a single door per side and like the H & B vans has sanding gear. In LNER days all brake vans were painted red oxide whether fitted or not.

Plate 334

Plate 335

A lighter GN brake van was the 13 ton type with outside framing illustrated in plate 335 of No. 418036, fresh in its new LNER livery late in 1923. The stove chimney in front of the interior oil lamp top on the roof and the side mounted riding lamp should be noted.

Figure 82 shows the diagram for the GN 4 wheeled 20 ton brake van, 245 of which were taken into LNER stock and 76 remained at nationalisation.

Figure 82

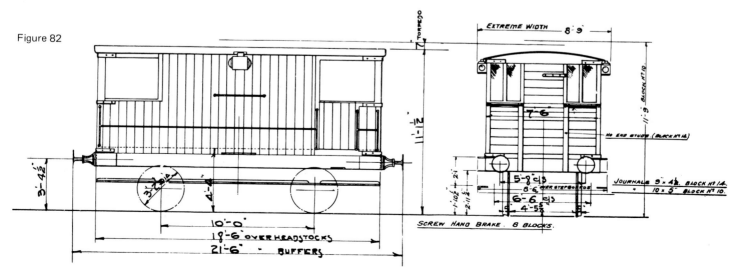

Figure 83

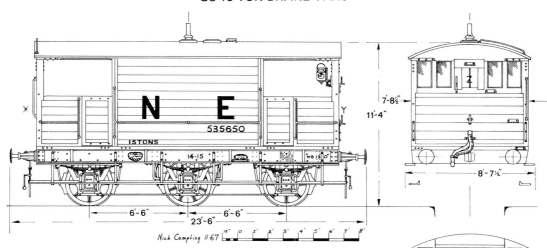

Figure 83 and plate 336 are of the GC 15 ton 6 wheel brake van produced in considerable numbers since 1903 at Dukinfield and by outside contractors. Most had steel underframes, but a timber version was built, while others were increased to 20 tons in weight. On figure 83 end 'X' is as drawn in the end view, while end 'Y' is similar but without steps or handrail. In the end view 'Z' denotes a two-plank door which was to enable the guard to change tail lamps. On the 'Y' end only the lamps as drawn could be swung out for travelling.

No. 509533 in plate 336 was built at Dukinfield in 1911 and photographed at Eastfield in January 1947.

Plate 336

Plate 337

The same design of brake van was supplied to the Cheshire Lines Committee and plate 337 shows No. 4481 constructed at Dukinfield in 1914 and seen here at Parkhead in March 1950.

Plate 338 illustrates a vacuum brake fitted van No. 509494 at Kings Cross in 1938. The curved brake pipe and hose can just be seen behind the buffer with the screw coupling below.

Plate 338

GE 20 TON BRAKE VAN

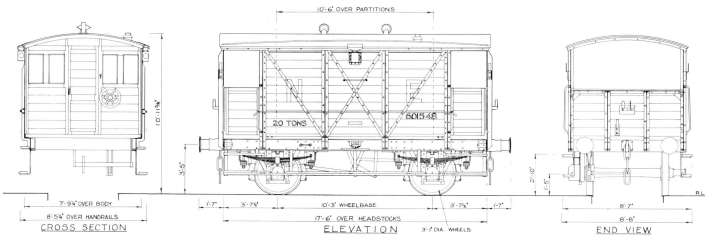

CROSS SECTION

10'-6" OVER PARTITIONS

7'-9¼" OVER BODY
8'-5¼" OVER HANDRAILS

10'-11⅝"

3'-5"

ELEVATION

1'-7"   3'-7½"   10'-3" WHEELBASE   3'-7½"   1'-7"
17'-6" OVER HEADSTOCKS
3'-1" DIA. WHEELS

END VIEW

8'-7"
8'-8"

2'-10"
1'-5"

R L

Plate 339

Figure 84

Plate 340

In 1904 the GE introduced its only 6 wheeled design of brake van of substantial construction weighing 20 tons and by 1908 fifty had been built. From this time on however until 1924 further brake vans were produced basically similar, but mounted on a 4 wheeled underframe, as shown in figure 84 and plates 339 and 340. The first photograph is of No. 601625 in BR livery at St. Ives (Hunts) in July 1953. Note the replacement buffer housings with thick wooden packing between them and the headstock, while the drawing and the other photograph are of vans fitted with self contained buffers. The hand brake wheel can be seen in the cross section on the drawing. One wheel was provided on each verandah on the same side of the vehicle and connected by a horizontal shaft running right through the van. From this bevel gears drove a vertical shaft, worm and crank, which in turn actuated the pull rods and brake shoes.

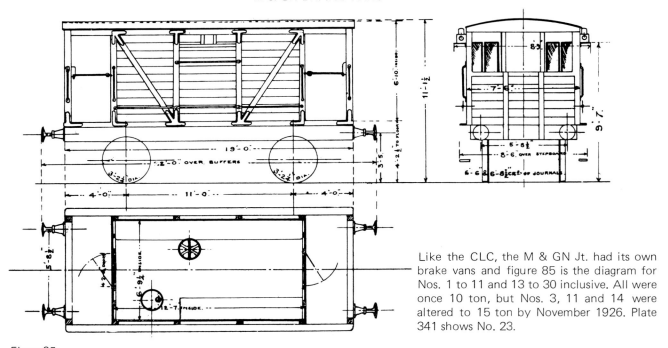

Figure 85

Like the CLC, the M & GN Jt. had its own brake vans and figure 85 is the diagram for Nos. 1 to 11 and 13 to 30 inclusive. All were once 10 ton, but Nos. 3, 11 and 14 were altered to 15 ton by November 1926. Plate 341 shows No. 23.

Plate 341

NB 10 TON BRAKE VANS

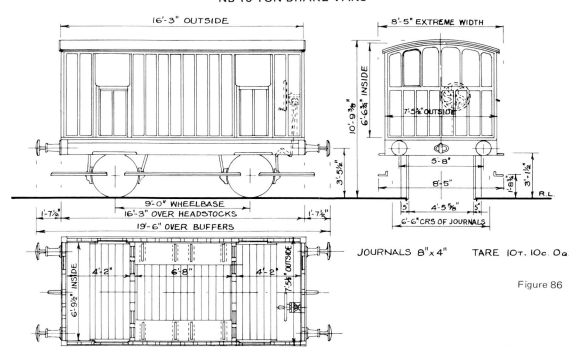

16'-3" OUTSIDE

8'-5" EXTREME WIDTH

10'-9⅜"

6'-6¾" INSIDE

7'-5½" OUTSIDE

3'-5½"

5'-8"

8'-5"

1'-8¾"

3'-1½"

R.L.

9'-0" WHEELBASE

16'-3" OVER HEADSTOCKS

19'-6" OVER BUFFERS

1'-7½"

1'-7½"

5'

4'-5⅝"

5'

6'-6" CRS OF JOURNALS

4'-2"

6'-8"

4'-2"

6'-9½" INSIDE

7'-5¾" OUTSIDE

JOURNALS 8" x 4"   TARE 10T. 10c. 0q.

Figure 86

Moving north of the border we come to North British brakes. Figure 86 is a faithful tracing of the diagram for an early 10 ton brake van with panelled sides and ends; later similar brakes were built with match board sides. A brake wheel was provided at one end in the enclosed vestibule.

Probably even older still is the NB 10 ton van No. 700032 with a part boarded and part railed verandah at one end as depicted in plate 342. It was constructed at Cowlairs, had no diagram and, although photographed in 1936 or later, was extinct by 1939. The letters 'N' and 'E' are just discernible on the original photograph in the second and fourth upper panels.

Plate 342

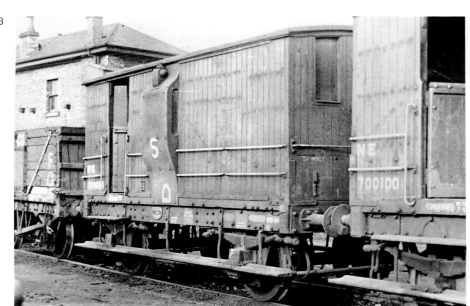

Plate 343

NB & GNS BRAKE VANS

The 17 ton brake van No. 700656 illustrated in plate 343 was built in 1923, but clearly of NB design with single vestibule and side duckets. It was withdrawn as seen here in June 1946.

The GNS 20 ton brake van shown in plate 344 and figure 87 is another late pregrouping design. The example in the photograph was made in 1924 and has been 'laid to rest' at Inverurie Works, her place of birth. Note that the lamp is still in position.

Plate 344

Figure 87

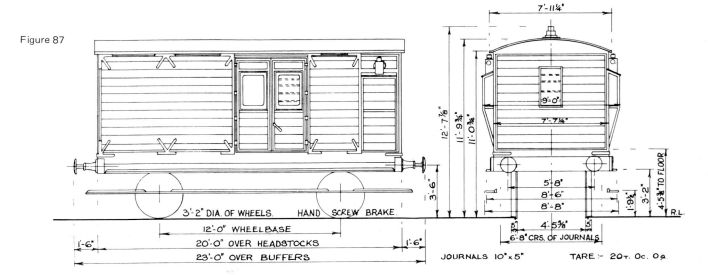

3'-2" DIA. OF WHEELS.   HAND SCREW BRAKE.

12'-0" WHEELBASE

20'-0" OVER HEADSTOCKS

23'-0" OVER BUFFERS

JOURNALS 10"x5"   TARE :- 20T. 0c. 0q.

Plate 345

The LNER's first design of brake van was the 'Toad B' illustrated in plates 345 and 346. No. 151752 was built at Dukinfield in 1927 and No. 153571 at Doncaster a year later. Note the variations in plank width and buffer housings on the two vehicles. Both are equipped with sanding gear and three hole disc wheels. A reinforced concrete version was even tried, but following complaints from the guards the idea was not pursued.

Plate 346

LNER 20 TON BRAKE VANS 'TOAD B AND E'

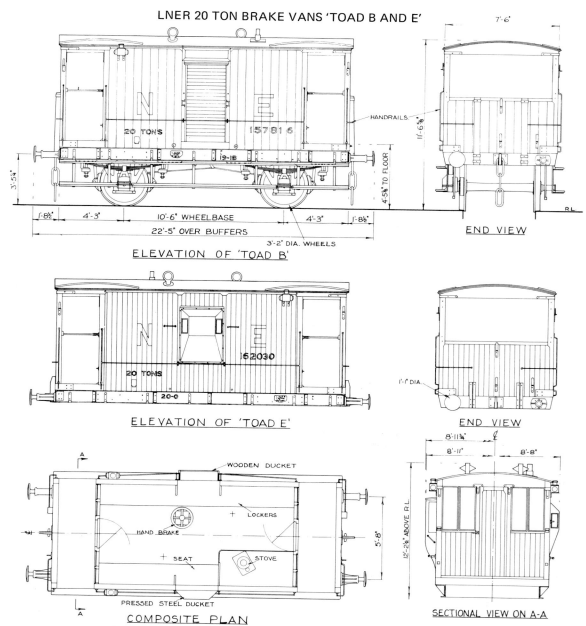

HANDRAILS

7'-6"

11'-6⅝"

4'-5⅞" TO FLOOR

R.L.

END VIEW

3'-5¼"

1'-8½" 4'-3" 10'-6" WHEELBASE 4'-3" 1'-8½"

22'-5" OVER BUFFERS

3'-2" DIA. WHEELS

ELEVATION OF 'TOAD B'

N E

20 TONS 157816 19-18

N E

162030

20 TONS 20-0

ELEVATION OF 'TOAD E'

1'-1" DIA.

END VIEW

A

WOODEN DUCKET

LOCKERS

HAND BRAKE

SEAT STOVE

PRESSED STEEL DUCKET

A

5'-8"

COMPOSITE PLAN

Figure 88

8'-11¾"

8'-11" 8'-8"

12'-2½" ABOVE R.L.

SECTIONAL VIEW ON A-A

N

Figure 88 is a composite drawing for the 'Toad B' and 'Toad E'. The first had the timber ducket, a close-up of which appears in plate 347, and the second the pressed steel version. In addition to this a host of other variations were incorporated into these vans, such as the width of planks and buffer housings already mentioned on the previous page; long wooden or short steel tee section end stanchions and three hole or spoked wheels were to be found. A few were equipped with automatic brake gear for special duties such as the workings down into Tyne Dock, but this was the exception rather than the rule.

Plate 347

Plate 348　　　　　　　　　　　LNER 20 TON BRAKE VANS 'TOAD E AND D'

A 'Toad E' in its final form is to be seen in plate 348. No. 175613 was registered at Darlington in 1934, having probably been built at Shildon, where it was photographed.

To obtain a smoother ride at the tail end of long distance express goods trains, the LNER had introduced a sample long wheel base van in 1929. The initial twenty were al-

located to the Kings Cross, Edinburgh and Aberdeen; Marylebone, York and Glasgow; York and Niddrie West; Liverpool and Newcastle services, and fish trains from Hull to Banbury and Kings Cross. At first these place names were painted on the van sides below the ducket. Plate 349 shows No. 182922 introduced into traffic in 1936.

Plate 349

LNER 20 TON BRAKE VAN 'TOAD D'

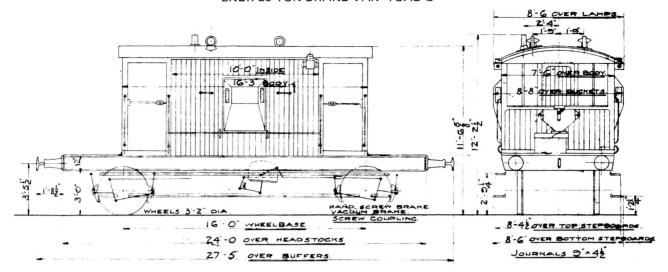

Figure 89

Plate 350

Figure 89 is a copy of diagram 61 for the 'Toad D'. As can be seen they were initially equipped with sanding gear, but this was removed by 1936 from all brake vans.

Plate 350 depicts No. 178705 registered at Darlington in 1935 and fitted with spoked wheels at the time of being photographed at Romsey in July 1950 in BR colours. The 'Toad D' design was later adopted by British Railways for their own standard brake van.

All 'Toad Ds' made for the LNER had automatic vacuum brake gear, but as plate 351 demonstrates the CLC were supplied in 1936 with some brake vans with hand brake only.

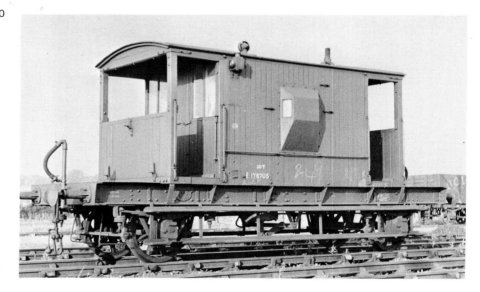

Plate 351

Plate 352

A few modifications to the design will be noticed in plates 352 and 353 of later 'Toad Ds', such as the raised end platform necessitated by the use of concrete as ballast instead of iron, owing to the scarcity of the latter during the war, and the small angle iron truss on the underside of the solebar. Roofs were then being painted the same colour as the bodysides. No. 260922 was built in 1944 and No. 278704 in 1946. Notice the 'Not to go' label in the label clip; presumably the vehicle was held back from entering traffic to have its photograph taken, and the two lamp brackets on the end instead of the three mounted on earlier vans.

Plate 353

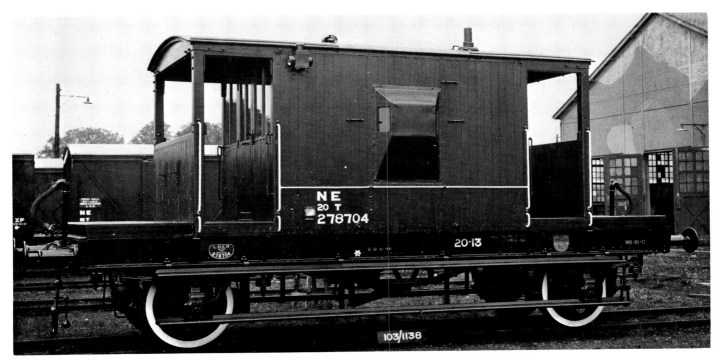

ACKNOWLEDGEMENTS

As has been hinted in the Preface this book has not been completed without a great deal of assistance from both members of the LNER Study Group and others, who have freely given of their time and loaned material. In particular thanks are due to Messrs. J.B. Dawson, P.N. Hall, J.R. Johnson, A.A. Maclean, R. Shepherd and J. Watling for making available information from their archives.

Gathering together the initial collection of photographs has not been helped by the fact that official views of LNER subjects have not been available from British Railways for a number of years and it is only through the generous help of Messrs. R. Chorley, R.J. Essery (for access to the collection of the late W.O. Steel) F. Newman and R.A. Woods that such a representative sample has been possible. Apart from those listed below all plates have been prepared from these official photographs:-

British Steel Corporation: 225

J.C. Dean collection: 43, 131, 132, 246, 266 and 330.

A.G. Ellis collection: 69, 90, 106, 115, 260, 261, 319, 336, 337 and 343.

R.R. Farrant: 211 and 212.

G. Y. Hemingway (courtesy Historical Model Railway Society): 11, 13, 14, 15, 18, 20, 21, 22, 24, 25, 26, 29, 44, 45, 49, 52, 54, 55, 56, 58, 75, 99, 103, 107, 108, 109, 118, 119, 161, 163, 178, 179, 230, 231, 257, 258, 259, 267, 268, 272, 273, 274, 276, 281, 284, 286, 288, 295, 299, 308, 329, 331, 332, 333, 338, 341 and 347.

Hurst Nelson (courtesy Motherwell Public Library): 28, 192, 196, 216 and 251.

J.R. Johnson collection: 1, 3 and 143.

A.A. Maclean collection: 232 and 344.

Metro-Cammell Ltd.: 199.

Real Photographs: 318.

Redpath Dorman Long Ltd.: 39, 42 and 113.

J.H. Russell: 6, 10, 40, 46, 59, 61, 207, 208, 213, 219, 245, 254 and 263.

W.O. Steel collection (courtesy of R.J. Essery): 27 and 342.

J. Templeton: 309, 315, 316 and 317.

J. Watling: 340.

A.E. West: 9, 17, 23, 33, 38, 57, 60, 66, 70, 77, 79, 92, 93, 98, 100, 101, 105, 112, 140, 152, 172, 175, 183, 193, 194, 197, 210, 214, 275, 278, 307, 314, 322, 324, 339 and 350.

N. Wilkinson: 313.

Author's collection: 310, 312, 320, 321 and 323.

Author: 2, 4, 5, 121, 127, 200, 290, 292, 293, 301, 303, 304 and 311.

Likewise with the exception of the following all the figures are attributable to British Railways:-

N.H. Campling: 20, 29 and 83.

M.J. Cook: 8, 28 and 64.

Institution of Mechanical Engineers (Railway Division): 4.

J. Watling: 13.

Author: 1, 2, 3, 9, 14, 15, 17, 21, 22, 23, 24, 25, 36, 49, 53, 54, 65, 66, 67, 68, 70, 75, 76, 84, 86, 87 and 88.

Figures 24 and 25 were prepared from original material kindly loaned by the Norfolk Railway Society, while figures 75 and 76 were developed from drawings supplied by the Craven Division of Messrs. Herbert Morris Ltd.

Finally thanks go to my two typists Alex and Marion, who have been generous enough to remark that typing the manuscript made a welcome relief from their other more mundane duties.

ERRATUM & ADDENDUM

Page 19, plate 31; page 39, plates 76 and 77; and page 46, plate 91.

Despite the inscription painted on their solebars, Nos 173575, 168848 and 168975 were some of the first wagons to have their wheelbase increased from 9 to 10 feet and it appears that at the time of applying the lettering the signwriter had yet to be informed! The number of the van in plate 77 also now seems uncertain.

Page 158, Plate 335.

Brake van No 418036 with outside framing does not conform with any of the GN diagrams and it has been suggested that the vehicle may have been taken over by the LNER from the East and West Yorkshire Union Railway on its absorption at grouping. It had formerly been owned jointly by the GN and Midland railways, but generally only used by the former. It would therefore be natural to number any vehicles in the GN list.

BIBLIOGRAPHY

Essery, R.J., Rowland, D.P. and Steel, W.O. *British Goods Wagon from 1887 to the present day.* David & Charles, Newton Abbot, 1970.

Foster, C. 'Mineral Wagons of the NER'. *The Journal of the Historical Model Railway Society,* 82. Vol. 7. 1970-72.

Hoole, K. 'NER Steam Breakdown Cranes and their Successors', *North Eastern Express,* Journal of the NER Association, Nos. 39 and 41.

Hoole, K. and Mallon, J. *North Eastern Railway Diagrams of Snow Ploughs,* Nidd Valley Narrow Gauge Railway, Knaresborough, 1969.

Newsome, N. 'The Development of LNER Carriage and Wagon Design, 1923-1941', *Journal of the Institution of Locomotive Engineers,* 420-483, Paper No. 477, Vol. 203, 1948.

'North Eastern Railway. Latest Developments in the Locomotive, Carriage and Wagon Departments. Wagon Stock', *The Locomotive,* 1913 and 1914.

'*How the LNER Carries Exceptional Freight Loads',* LNER, 1931.

APPENDIX I

FREIGHT STOCK ABSORBED BY LNER

Type	Load Capacity	NER inc. H & BR	GNR	GCR	GER	NBR	GNSR	Total
Open Goods Wagons	under 8T	669	114	—	—	18	—	801
	8T to under 10T	4,417	17,240)				) 2,583	
	10T to under 12T	9,520	8,843)	) 19,455	) 18,291	) 13,169	)	120,927
	12T	26,309	1,100)	)	)	)	—	
	over 12T to under 20T	—	361	—	—	—	42	403
	20T & over (bogie)	56	26	—	—	—	—	82
	TOTAL	40,971	27,684	19,455	18,291	13,187	2,625	122,213
Covered Goods Vans	under 8T	849	939	88	47	242	66	2,231
	8T to under 10T	291	3,115)		) 5,264	) 4,031	) 499	
	10T to under 12T	2,356	4)	) 2,827	)	)	)	) 24,743
	12T	6,354	2)	)	—	—	—	)
	over 12T to under 20T	417	—	231	—	100	—	748
	20T and over (bogie)	101	1	—	—	—	—	102
	TOTAL	10,368	4,061	3,146	5,311	4,373	565	27,824
Mineral Wagons	under 8T	92	—	—	—	67	—	159
	8T to under 10T	488	1,242)	)	)	)	—	)
	10T to under 12T	25,293	2,323)	) 8,425	) 175	) 22,406	—	) 70,706
	12T	10,354	—)	)	)	)	—	)
	over 12T to under 20T	2,159	569	—	—	12,300	—	15,028
	20T & over (ordinary)	18,206	300	—	—	—	—	18,506
	20T & over (bogie)	100	—	—	—	—	—	100
	TOTAL	56,692	4,434	8,425	175	34,773	—	104,499
GRAND TOTAL (Open, Covered & Mineral)		108,031	36,179	31,026	23,777	52,333	3,190	254,536
Special wagons (ordinary)		)	300	) 348	200	) 129	—	) 1,207
Special wagons (bogie)		) 220	6	)	4	)	—	)
Cattle trucks		2,150	673	381	1,653	1,719	262	6,838
Rail & timber trucks (ordinary)		11,928	684	) 2,689	979	) 930	79	) 17,461
Rail & timber trucks (bogie)		172	—	)	—	)	—	)
Miscellaneous		—	—	—	—	13	1	14
TOTAL (excluding brake vans)		122,501	37,842	34,444	26,613	55,124	3,532	280,056
Brake vans	10T to 15T		366	866	295			
	over 15T		505	20	305			
	TOTAL	1,322	871	886	600	682	71	4,432
GRAND TOTAL (Merchandise & Mineral)		123,823	38,713	35,330	27,213	55,806	3,603	284,488
Service Stock								
Ballast Wagons & Ballast Brakes		1,171	800	405	572	264	74	3,286
Breakdown Cranes		21	18	16	10	3	2	70
Coal, Coke, Ash & Sand Wagons		2,151	1,421	2,399	2,084	2,669	27	10,751
Gas Holder Trucks		19	45	14	48	12	—	138
Mess & Tool Vans		404	55	19	26	96	2	602
Travelling Cranes		58	47	16	25	10	1	157
Miscellaneous		132	482	94	126	110	18	962
TOTAL		3,956	2,868	2,963	2,891	3,164	124	15,966
Shunt Horses		160	110	44	264	—	—	578

NOTE: Appendices 1, 2 and 3 are offered to give readers an idea of the overall proportions of the LNER's wagon stock and to indicate trends during the period under review. The figures quoted should not be relied upon to the final digit, as the Company itself was not exactly certain how many vehicles it had in stock at any given time and small discrepancies may be found between figures taken from differential sources.

APPENDIX 2

PREGROUPING FREIGHT STOCK REMAINING ON THE LNER

Type	Load Capacity	NER		H & B		GN		GC		GE		NB		GNS	
	Year ending 31st Dec.	1940	1947	1940	1947	1940	1947	1940	1947	1940	1947	1940	1947	1940	1947
Open goods wagon	under 8T	205	47	1	—	3	2	—	—	—	—	49	12	2	—
	8T to under 10T	19	7	—	—	1,071	176	271	71	—	—	750	106	143	15
	10T to under 12T	55	21	525	93	8,361	4,289	2,915	872	3,031	1,209	588	135	43	19
	12T	20,410	8,925	—	—	986	692	1,532	661	—	—	11	10	—	—
	over 12T to under 20T	—	—	—	—	336	175	—	—	—	—	213	60	—	—
	20T & over (bogie)	—	—	—	—	26	26	—	—	—	—	—	—	—	—
	TOTAL	20,689	9,000	526	93	10,783	5,360	4,718	1,604	3,031	1,209	1,611	323	188	34
Covered goods vans	under 8T	61	19	41	19	203	72	35	21	—	—	220	33	—	—
	8T to under 10T	1	1	6	3	1,993	1,377	12	8	—	—	309	88	—	—
	10T to under 12T	1,052	689	47	20	345	321	1,829	1,097	3,112	2,715	2,376	1,236	18	1
	12T	3,988	1,935	—	—	—	—	132	10	—	—	—	—	340	238
	over 12T to under 20T	57	24	—	—	—	—	10	—	—	—	99	47	—	—
	20T & over (bogie)	101	94	—	—	—	—	—	—	—	—	—	—	—	—
	TOTAL	5,260	2,762	94	42	2,541	1,770	2,018	1,136	3,112	2,715	3,004	1,404	358	239
Mineral wagons	8T to under 10T	—	—	—	—	2,428	468	—	—	—	—	5,939	648	1	—
	10T to under 12T	3,591	642	—	—	1,121	641	806	205	2	1	445	148	—	—
	12T	8,714	4,282	—	—	—	—	742	608	—	—	138	74	—	—
	over 12T to under 20T	500	100	—	—	450	181	—	—	—	—	8,277	5,162	—	—
	20T & over (ordinary)	13,984	6,054	—	—	—	—	—	—	—	—	—	—	—	—
	20T & over (bogie)	59	—	—	—	—	—	—	—	—	—	—	—	—	—
	TOTAL	26,848	11,078	—	—	3,999	1,290	1,548	813	2	1	14,799	6,032	1	—
GRAND TOTAL (open, covered & mineral)		52,797	22,840	620	135	17,323	8,420	8,284	3,553	6,145	3,925	19,414	7,759	547	273
Special wagons (ordinary)		122	97	—	—	165	76	205	153	140	111	81	27	1	1
Special wagons (bogie)		364	341	—	—	6	6	42	37	1	—	29	25	—	—
Cattle trucks		728	213	1	—	199	96	114	44	412	59	462	62	58	3
Rail & timber trucks (ordinary)		7,249	4,358	68	19	239	134	1,590	1,212	279	154	324	133	10	8
TOTAL (excluding brake vans)		61,260	27,849	689	154	17,932	8,732	10,235	4,999	6,977	4,249	20,310	8,006	616	285
Brake vans	10T to 15T	502	293	5	2	1	—	407	256	1	—	94	3	26	—
	over 15T	8	—	41	28	427	267	17	13	357	263	153	40	6	6
	TOTAL	510	293	46	30	428	267	424	269	358	263	247	43	32	6
GRAND TOTAL (merchandise & mineral)		61,770	28,142	735	84	18,360	8,999	10,659	5,268	7,355	4,512	20,557	8,049	648	291
Loco Coal		1,214	288	98	36	921	148	357	61	971	732	1,133	478	258	142
Sleeper		2,294	1,183	—	—	1,002	24	38	15	—	—	—	—	—	—

CENSUS OF FREIGHT STOCK OF LNER

Type	Load Capacity	Year 1929	Year 1938	Year 1947
Open Goods Wagons	Under 8T	43	21	2
	8T to under 10T	17,912	6,275	998
	10T to under 12T	45,883	21,504	7,670
	12T (up to 14T later)	58,229	77,932	78,208
	over 12T to under 20T	639	484	191
	20T & over (ordinary)	200	275	290
	20T & over (bogie)	27	132	131
	TOTAL	122,933	106,623	90,549
Covered Goods Vans	under 8T	1,585	467	119
	8T to under 10T	4,158	2,845	1,899
	10T to under 12T	11,990	9,738	8,181
	12T	13,458	27,702	40,635
	over 12T to under 20T	467	178	72
	20T & over (ordinary)	25	—	—
	20T & over (bogie)	102	101	94
	TOTAL	31,785	41,031	51,000
·Mineral Wagons	under 8T	22	1	—
	8T to under 10T	13,052	5,609	401
	10T to under 12T	16,122	8,623	1,369
	12T (up to 14T later)	21,819	27,144	31,222
	over 12T to under 20T	15,260	11,606	13,684
	20T & over (ordinary)	23,496	25,529	24,885
	20T & over (bogie)	143	113	24
	TOTAL	89,914	78,625	71,585
GRAND TOTAL (Open, Covered & Mineral)		244,632	226,279	210,075
Special Wagons	(Ordinary)	2,769	7,190	9,009
Special Wagons	(Bogie)	464	760	809
Cattle Trucks		7,033	4,884	2,560
Rail & Timber Trucks	(Ordinary)	13,063	13,476	13,426
	(Bogie)	549	976	987
	TOTAL (excluding brake vans)	268,510	253,566	236,866
Brake Vans	10T to 15T	2,513	1,306	720
	over 15T	2,005	3,364	3,979
	TOTAL	4,518	4,670	4,699
GRAND TOTAL Merchandise & Mineral		273,028	258,236	241,565
Average Age (years)		16.51	16.62	16.25
Containers In Stock		685	4,286	5,202
Average Age			3.82	9.64
Service Stock				
Ballast Wagons & Ballast Brake Vans		2,515	1,627	1,561
Breakdown Cranes		66	56	57
Coal, Coke, Ash & Sand Wagons		10,826	7,585	5,128
Gas Holder Trucks		144	153	146
Mess & Tool Vans		677	645	686
Timber, Rail & Sleeper Trucks		198	113	90
Travelling Cranes		226	214	219
Miscellaneous		901	1,318	1,423
	TOTAL	15,553	11,711	9,310

LNER FREIGHT STOCK CODES

Description	Code	
Armour plate wagon	ARM (A to K)	S
Ash or rubbish wagon	BLUE	
Ballast wagon — under 20 tons capacity	ED	
20 tons capacity	EDL	
Ballast/rail bogie wagons — 30 tons capacity & over	BALLAST	
Ballast plough brake vans	TOAD PLOUGH	
Banana Van	BANANA	L
Bar iron wagon	BAR	
Bell wagon	BELL	S
Boiler wagons — boiler (flat)	BOILER (A to J)	S
twin boiler (flat)	TWIN BOILER (A to F)	S
locomotive boiler	BOILER (K)	S
Bolster wagons — single	SINGLE	
twin	TWIN	
double	DOUBLE	
treble (bogie)	TREBLE	S
quadruple (bogie)	QUAD	S
quintuple (bogie)	QUINT (A to D)	S
septuple (bogie)	SEPT	S
swivel bolsters (bogie)	GONDOLA	S
Brake van	TOAD	
Brick wagon	BRICK	S
Cask wagon	CASK	
Cattle trucks — ordinary	MEX (later OX)	
fitted with automatic brake or pipe	MEXFIT (later OXFIT)	
Coke wagons — up to 12 tons capacity	COKE	L
14 tons capacity	COMBINE	
Conduit wagons	CONDUIT	
Containers — small covered	BOX A	
large covered	BOX B	
small open	BOX C	
large open	BOX D	
Container flat wagon	CONFLAT	L
Covered goods vans — ordinary up to 12 tons capacity	COVAN	
ordinary up to 15 tons capacity	TRAVAN	
fitted with automatic brake or pipe up to 12 tons capacity	COVFIT	
Economiser wagon	MISER	S
Egg wagon	EGG	
End door mineral wagons — N.E. & Southern area (all capacities)	END or END DOOR	
Scottish areas — up to 12 tons capacity	END	
over 12 tons capacity	LAREND	
Fish trucks — open	FISHO	L
covered 4 wheels	FISHCOV	P
covered 6 wheels	XFISH	P
covered bogie	BOFISH	P
Flat wagons	FLAT (A to U)	S
Fruit vans fitted with automatic brake or pipe up to 12 tons capacity	FRUIT	P
Gas tanks — single	GAS SINGLE	
double	GAS DOUBLE	
triple	GAS TRIPLE	
Glass wagons — stanchion	GLASS A	S
well	WELL GLASS (B to O)	S
Gunpowder van	POWDER (A to J)	S
Gunset	GUNSET	S

Wagon type	Code	
High-sided open wagons (sides over 2 feet) —		
ordinary	HIGH	
fitted with automatic brake or pipe	HYFIT or OFIT	
long fitted with automatic brake	LONGFIT	L
Bogie 30 tons capacity	30 TON GOODS	S
Hopper bottom door wagons — 10½ tons capacity	X	
15-17 tons capacity	XV	
20 tons capacity	XX	
30 tons capacity	XXX	
40 tons capacity (bogie)	XXXX	
with end brakes up to 12 tons capacity	STRIPE	
bulk aluminium	ALUMINA	L
ballast stone 25 tons capacity	STONE BALLAST	
bulk grain	GRAIN	L
ironstone	IRON	
railed coke	RAIL	
soda ash	SODA ASH	L
Locomotive coal wagons — 10 tons capacity	X LOCO	L
15 tons capacity	XV LOCO	L
20 tons capacity	XX LOCO	L
30 tons capacity	XXX LOCO	L
40 tons capacity	XXXX LOCO	L
Lowsided goods wagons (sides 2 ft. or less) — ordinary	LOW	
fitted with automatic brake	LOWFIT	L
Machine wagons — high machine (ramped)	IMP (A to X)	S
low machine (ramped)	MAC (A to P)	S
twin machine (ramped)	TWIN IMP (A to C)	S
rectank (ramped)	RECTANK (A and B)	S
traction engine	TRACTION (B to D)	S
Match wagon	MATCH	
Perishable van fitted with automatic brake or pipe up to 12 tons capacity	PERISH	L
Pig iron wagon	PIG	L
Plate wagons — 4 wheels up to 12 tons capacity	PLATE	L
4 wheels 20 tons capacity	LAPLATE	L
6 wheels	XPLATE	L
bogie	BOPLATE (A to E)	S
trestle	TRESTLE (A to N)	S
Propellor wagon (air screws)	AERO	
Pulley wagons — wheel	PULLEY (A to C)	S
pulley	PULLEY (D to L)	S
Refrigerator wagons — without ventilating apparatus	REFRIG	L
with ventilating apparatus	VENTREFRIG	L
Rubbish or ash wagons	BLUE	
Salt wagon	SALT	L
Sugar beet wagon	SUGAR	
Sulphate (bogie)	SULPHATE	S
Sleeper wagon	SLEEP	L
Toy continental wagon	TOY	
Transformer	TRANSFORMER	S
Trolley wagons — flat	FLATROL (A to Z and AA-DD)	S
open well (removable crossbars)	WELTROL (A to T)	S
propellor	PROTROL (A to G)	S
trestle	TRESTROL (A to C)	S
Tube wagon	TUBE	L
Vegetable wagon	VEG	
Yeast wagon	YEAST	
Rope	ROPE	
Wagon sheet	SHEET	

Notes

1. 'L' in right hand column indicates that the code name or part of it was painted on the wagon side. 'P' indicates that a small cast iron plate bearing the code was attached to the side of the vehicle. All specially constructed vehicles had their code in full painted on them and these are denoted by the letter 'S'. For further details see page 96.

2. Fish trucks although numbered in the wagon series and included in the freight stock diagram books were classed as non-passenger coaching stock.

STEAM BREAKDOWN CRANES OF LONDON, NORTH EASTERN RAILWAY

Pregroup Coy & No.	LNER No. '38 Scheme	BR No.	Max. Cap.	Maker	Works/ Order No.	Year Built	Wheel Arrang.	Match Wagon No.	Allocation c.1926	c.1937	Nov. 1947	Present Status 4/75	Remarks
NER 1	901626	(331)151	35T	Cowans	3335	1916	4-6-0		Gateshead	York	York	Withdrawn '68	2T Aux.hoist
NER 2	901627	—	15T	Cowans	1859	1893	4-4-0		Tweedmouth	Tweedmouth	Shildon C&W '38	Withdrawn	
NER 3	901628	155	15T	Cowans	2118	1898	4-4-0		Sunderland		W.Hartlepool	Withdrawn '58	
— 5	901630	(331)158	35T	Cowans	6080	1937	4-8-4RB	901715/2111	—	Tweedmth. 10/37	Tweedmouth	Withdrawn '72	
NER 12	901637	152	25T	Craven	8153	1907	2-4-2	901701	Darlington	Darlington	Sunderland	Withdrawn c.60	
NER 13	901638	(331)153	25T	Craven	8153	1907	2-4-2		Middlesbrough	Middlesbrough	Middlesbrough	Preserved	
NER 14	901639	(331)157	25T	Craven	8153	1907	2-4-2	901711	Dairycoates	Dairycoates	Dairycoates	Withdrawn c.62	
— 22	901646	154	45T	Cowans	4525	1926	4-0-4	24163	Gateshead '26	Gateshead	Gateshead	Withdrawn '68	
—	901719	(331)156	45T	Cowans	6872	1940	4-8-4RB	901720		Darlington '40	Darlington	Extant Thornaby	
SB1/39A	941590	(330)107	45T	Cowans	4524	1926	4-0-4	39AA/ 941751	Doncaster '26	Doncaster	Doncaster	Extant Healey Mills	
—	941591	124	36T	Cowans	5755	1936	4-8-4RB	941753	—		Colwick	Extant Toton	(6T Aux.hoist LMR RS1106/36)
GN A343	941592	123	35T	Craven	9780	1914	2-6-2		Doncaster	New England	Woodford Halse	Withdrawn 4/66	LMR RS 1096/35
GE 6A	941593	54 (WR)	35T	Rapier	B7478	1915	0-6-4		King's Cross	King's Cross	Neasden	Withdrawn	LMR RS 1095/35
SB 9	941594	109	15T	Cowans		1898	4-4-0				Grantham	Withdrawn '61	
GN 152A	941595	106	15T	Cowans	2247	1899	4-4-0				Lincoln	Withdrawn '55	
GN	941596	—	15T	Smith		1892	0-6-0				—	Withdrawn	
—	941599	(330)110	45T	Cowans	6871	1940	4-8-4RB	941765	—	New Eng. 2/40	New England	Extant March	
—	941600	—	45T	Cowans	6875	1940	4-8-4RB	941766	—	King's Cross '40	—	To War Dept.	
—	941601	(330)102	45T	Rapier	F4991/3	1943	4-8-4RB	941767			King's Cross	Extant Tinsley	
GC	951501	105	20T	Craven	8138	1907	2-4-2		Gorton	Gorton	Darnall	Withdrawn	
GN	951502	108	15T	Smith		1892	0-6-0				Grimsby	Withdrawn	
GC	951503	121	15T	Cowans	2121	1898	4-4-0				Mexborough	Withdrawn '58	
MS & L	951504	125	15T	Cowans		1893	4-4-0	951663			Langwith Jct.	Withdrawn c.65	
GC	951505	104	15T	Cowans	2119	1898	4-4-0				Hornsey	Withdrawn	
GC	951506	101	15T	Cowans	2120	1898	4-4-0				Ardsley	Withdrawn	
—	951515	—	45T	Cowans	6874	1940	4-8-4RB	951675	—	Gorton '40	—	To War Dept.	
—	951516	122	45T	Rapier	F4991/3	1943	4-8-4RB	951676	—		Gorton	Extant Newton Heath	LMR RS 1083/45
GER 1A		—	10T			1885	0-6-0		Cambridge		—	built as hand & converted to steam	Downrated from 12T 11/18
GER 2A		—	10T			1885	0-6-0		Peterborough E		—		
GER 3A		—	12T				0-6-0		Kings Lynn		—		
GER SB4	961600	135	35T	Rapier	C413	1919	0-6-4		Stratford	Stratford	Thorpe '40	Withdrawn c.68	
—	961601	(330)131	35T	Rapier	D4648	1932	4-8-4RB	961652		Cambridge	Stratford	Withdrawn 3/70	
GER 4A	961602	134	20T	GER	—	1908	0-8-0				March	Withdrawn c.64	
GER 5A	961603	132	20T	GER	—	1908	0-8-0				Ipswich	Withdrawn '67	
GN 150A	961604	—	15T	Cowans	2246	1899	4-4-0	961658		Norwich	Colchester	Withdrawn '54	
	961605						0-6-0	961659			—	Withdrawn	
—	961606	(330)133	45T	Cowans	6873	1940	4-8-4RB	961665	—	Cambridge '40	Cambridge	Extant Cambridge	
NB 770517	971567	RS 1062/36	36T	Cowans	3310	1914	4-4-4	770518 971568	St. Margarets	St. Margarets	St. Margarets	Extant Dundee	1TAux.hoist
NB 770539	971571	RS 1051/18	20T	Forrest		1882	0-6-0	770540 971572	Eastfield	Thornton Jct.	Bathgate (Uppr)	Withdrawn 9/64	
NER15, 770569	971569	RS 1063/35	35T	Craven	9372	1912	2-6-2	770570 971570	York	Eastfield 11/27	Thornton Jct.	Withdrawn '67	
—	971588	RS 1058/45	45T	Cowans	6870	1939	4-8-4RB	971589	—	Thornton Jct.1/40	Eastfield	Extant Eastfield	
NB 880044	981508		15T	Cowans	2117	1897	4-4-0	981509	Thornton Jct.	Kittybrewster	Kittybrewster	Withdrawn '50	

Notes

1. The full title of the manufacturers are as follows:-

   Cowans, Sheldon & Co. Ltd. of Carlisle.
   Ransomes & Rapier Ltd. of Ipswich.
   Craven Bros. of Manchester.
   T. Smith & Sons (Rodley) Ltd. of Leeds.
   Forrest & Co. of Port Dundas, Glasgow.
   Great Eastern Railway, Stratford Works.

2. The wheel arrangement is expressed in White's notation with the crane considered as normally leading with the jib in train formation. 'R.B.' indicates that detachable relieving bogies are fitted.

3. The LNER's departmental numbering scheme introduced in 1938 is described in broader context on page 6. Prior to this each Area perpetuated one of its pre-grouping company's schemes or devised its own to suit its needs. There is evidence that the Southern Area used the letters 'SB' followed by a number, but only a few between 1 and 9 have been found. The North Eastern Area continued its 'CME' list to incorporate cranes delivered up until 1937. While in Scotland cranes were numbered in the 770XXX and 880XXX series for the Southern and Northern Scottish Areas respectively.

4. The British Railways numbers on the Eastern and North Eastern Regions were allocated in 1954 and initially the last three digits only were used. Later the full number was carried and often prefixed 'DE'.

   After nationalisation those belonging to the Scottish Region were re-numbered in the LMS scheme, but, it should be noted, not without duplicating numbers of cranes remaining in use on the London Midland Region in certain instances.

INDEX